Linguanomics

Other Books by Gabrielle Hogan-Brun:

Linguanomics

WHAT IS THE MARKET POTENTIAL OF MULTILINGUALISM?

GABRIELLE HOGAN-BRUN

Bloomsbury Academic
An imprint of Bloomsbury Publishing Plc

B L O O M S B U R Y
LONDON · OXFORD · NEW YORK · NEW DELHI · SYDNEY

Bloomsbury Academic

An imprint of Bloomsbury Publishing Plc

50 Bedford Square
London
WC1B 3DP
UK

1385 Broadway
New York
NY 10018
USA

www.bloomsbury.com

**BLOOMSBURY and the Diana logo are trademarks
of Bloomsbury Publishing Plc**

First published 2017

British Library Cataloguing-in-Publication Data
A catalogue record for this book is available from the British Library.

ISBN: HB: 978-1-4742-3831-1
PB: 978-1-4742-3829-8
ePDF: 978-1-4742-3833-5
ePub: 978-1-4742-3832-8

Library of Congress Cataloging-in-Publication Data
A catalog record for this book is available from the Library of Congress.

Cover design: Louise Dugdale
Cover image © bgblue / Getty Images

Typeset by Deanta Global Publishing Services, Chennai, India

For John

CONTENTS

ACKNOWLEDGEMENTS

With thanks to: Bill Dale, Justin Dillon, Yoshiko Fujita, Richard Green, Terry Jones, Gurdeep Mattu, Mary Morris, Tony Morris, Valerio Rinaldi, Mary Stoate, Claire Thomson, The Hogans, especially Christopher, Sarah, Patrick and John.

SETTING THE SCENE

Polyglots, or at least bilinguals, wanted

You may have come across claims that language skills shortages harm the economy. But what are the facts? Consider the following statement:

> One in four UK and one in six US businesses [is] losing out due to lack of language skills and cultural awareness in their workforce.[1]

Corporations with international ambitions need multilingual employees to sell their goods and services. Many other organizations also require among their workforce people skilled in at least one non-native language. This need is reflected in today's hiring strategies. For example, the London Metropolitan Police is looking for bilingual recruits capable of forming a rapport with the city's diverse citizens to 'help boost confidence, solve crime more effectively and support victims and witnesses'.[2] The languages sought after range from Arabic and Punjabi to Yoruba.

> Following the introduction of the additional language eligibility criteria as a key skill to become a police constable in the Met, you must now be able to speak one of ... 25 languages to be eligible to apply. ... Unless you meet our eligibility criteria, you will be unable to submit an application at this time.[3]

Across the Atlantic, the US military requires officers who are proficient in languages critical to their national security –

currently Arabic, Chinese, Hindi, Indonesian, Korean, Persian, Portuguese, Russian, Swahili, Turkish and Urdu.

> Entitlement to Foreign Language Proficiency Pay is established for officers and enlisted members receiving basic pay and certified by the individual service secretary to be proficient in a foreign language or dialect.[4]

This initiative is generating new career paths as in the case of one student at the Portland State University Russian Flagship Program, who says: 'I am pursuing dual degrees in Russian and Architecture and plan to use my professional-level fluency to work as an architect for the US Army Corps of Engineers collaborating on projects with Russian speaking nations.'[5]

As these vignettes show, multilingual skills are valued by some employers and are economically favourable. But in the public sector, dealing with multilingualism is more often associated with costs. Financial constraints might mean that justice is more difficult to arrive at and that medical conditions are more difficult to diagnose. In severe cases, there might be miscarriages of justice, or misdiagnoses. This social dimension forms part of the pay-off when considering the costs and benefits of language diversity. Here too, multilingual individuals have a vital role to play.

On multilingualism

Multilingualism means different things in different places. It is estimated that half of the world's population is bilingual or multilingual. There are 6,000–7,000 languages in the world today, currently spread over just 196 countries. In many regions across the globe, a citizen's ability to speak multiple languages is therefore 'normal and quite unremarkable' and is an 'instrumental response to mundane needs'[6] in the life of a considerable percentage of people. They may use one language to communicate with government officials, another within their own family and possibly a third when buying and selling. They might not speak the languages they know equally well but will try to make themselves understood to get what they need. Among such language-rich territories are Papua New Guinea, Nigeria, India and South Africa.

But multilingual practice is not just a characteristic of a 'rainbow nation'. In the largely homogenized Western world, cultures are being brought together at an unprecedented rate through social mobility. Cheap air travel has encouraged tourism on a massive scale and migration has become easier for some. In addition, the Web is an open gateway for the exchange of information across the globe. In short, multilingualism is playing more of a role in many Western societies. But it has always existed and likely will continue to do so. As we shall see, our ancestors utilized it: first to help them survive, then to barter and to prosper. They learnt and created languages, too, as they traded across distances. All the time, their business and language practices went hand in hand. With today's growing language needs, the challenge is to understand and unearth the economic and social benefits of multilingualism.

In fact, we do not have to look very far. Many schools, organizations and cities feature various types of multilingualism. In some countries, for example Luxembourg and Switzerland, it is officially supported. What is more, economists have even studied exactly how much citizens can benefit from speaking more than one language. Since multilingualism has been found to be rewarding at both the personal and national levels, it has been exploited in both countries. But the picture is not all rosy. Too much multilingualism is not cost-effective; there is a sweet spot that lies somewhere between using only one language and using too many. In addition, as we shall see, there is clear evidence that deals can be missed and, in worst case scenarios, people's lives can be lost if multilingualism is not managed within the larger framework of multicultural understanding. So learning another language makes economic sense and will ultimately benefit individuals and society alike. It is already a practice across much of the European Union (EU), where children are taught two languages (in addition to their own) from an early age.

On Linguanomics

BBC News Wales reported (on 7 November 2014) that 'staff at Lidl supermarkets are being stopped from speaking any language other than English in their UK stores – including Welsh'. The store said it was to ensure that all their staff and customers 'felt comfortable'.[7] Following political and consumer pressure, the firm (a discount chain that is headquartered in Germany) then withdrew this policy, stating that 'it is a "great asset" to have such a multi-lingual workforce'.[8]

This story encapsulates the central message of this book. It shows that languages have market value and that language skills should be seen as assets. But the utility of a particular language tends to be linked to the number of speakers. This is why Lidl's managers considered English as more valuable than Welsh in their shops. However, this decision could have cost them the loyalty of their Welsh-speaking customers. As we shall see, this scenario is reflected on an international scale where corporations need to balance their language choices between global and local market forces.

Linguanomics has grown from my conviction that society can benefit from language diversity. It reflects insights from my own language trajectories and from my work on language planning and policy matters across the EU. I have always been driven by an understanding that multilingualism forms part of wider socio-political and economic issues and tensions therein. Here I lay out the facts for readers to make up their own minds about the interconnections of multilingualism and economics today.

CHAPTER ONE

Trading across cultures: Then and now

As soon as groups of our prehistoric ancestors began communicating with each other around 150,000 years ago, they started to barter. Trading across cultures in order to procure food or other resources is almost as old as people's need to survive. With the domestication of beasts of burden, and the improvement of transportation means by land and sea, trade links extended over longer and longer distances.

Early merchants had to be creative in order to communicate across cultures. They soon started to use words from the languages of their different suppliers to buy and sell, or seal a deal. As commercial networks widened, several trade languages became the primary vehicles of business interactions. With the growth of empires came the spread of languages, leaving an indelible mark on cultures across the globe.

There are contemporary parallels with the use of economically prevalent languages in international business. We can see this in modern entities such as the Association of Southeast Asian Nations Free Trade Area (AFTA), North American Free Trade Agreement (NAFTA) and the European Union (EU): trade and language going hand in hand, offering opportunities for expansion and development, provided that communication across languages and cultures is effective.

Today many of us still share our early ancestors' motives in using different languages to secure resources and to cooperate. It is just that our means of doing so have changed. This chapter traces the role of languages in trade through selective examples from antiquity to the present day. The Middle East is where organized trade was concentrated in early history, and it is well documented. So this is where the story starts.

Early trade and transportation

Ancient Egyptians were experts in embalming their deceased. They did so believing that their bodies were needed in the afterlife. The Greek historian Herodotus, writing in about 450 BC, describes their practice of preserving bodies as follows:

> There are … men in Egypt who practice the art of embalming, and make it their proper business. … [The] most perfect process is [to] draw out the brain through the nostrils…, take out the whole contents of the abdomen, which they then cleanse. … After this they fill the cavity with the purest bruised myrrh, with cassia … and sew up the opening.[1]

Intriguingly, these fragrant herbs, used to perfume the disembowelled corpses, did not grow in Egypt. Embalmers depended on others to import these products for their funeral rituals. Myrrh came from southern Arabia and the cassia bark was mainly harvested from trees that grow in East Asia. In addition, many Egyptian mummies were found with small pieces of amber inserted beneath the skin of their hands as a means of protection after death. Since antiquity, this desirable gemstone has been transported from the shores of the Baltic Sea, where the fossilized tree resin is swept up in abundance from the seabed.[2]

Egyptians had their own extensive trade routes centred on the Nile. To obtain exotic commodities from Africa and

Asia, they mostly relied on their sea-faring neighbours. Among their suppliers were the Phoenicians from the shores of modern-day Lebanon, who have gone down in history as an enterprising maritime trading culture. We know from Herodotus that they had the technology to build ships with a keeled hull to stabilize forward motion and provide ballast. From bases at the Egyptian Red Sea ports, they gradually pushed their commercial influence south along the African coast. Maritime transportation meant that cargoes could be moved in bulk, which lowered the cost of metals, construction materials and foodstuffs. Among their luxury imports were the skins of lions and leopards, and possibly also gold, whereas their exports included quality timber for shipbuilding and architecture, precious ivory and dyes. They are even believed to have collected tin from the British shores to trade in the Mediterranean.

How did the Phoenician traders take orders from their Egyptian clients? Since the main centres of Phoenician culture were nearby, it is likely that they picked up some elements of the Egyptian language to conduct business. But the story would have been different in the case of interactions with suppliers in faraway places such as Ethiopia, Somalia or Cornwall. With increasing distance, similarities between languages would have been harder to find, limiting the extent of communication that could be made. This situation is illustrated by Herodotus' account of a story he had heard about a journey taken by some Nasamonean Libyans into Central Africa. He writes that 'the Nasamoneans could not understand a word of their [hosts'] language, nor had [the hosts] any acquaintance of the language of the Nasamoneans'.[3] We do not know whether the Nasamoneans ended up trading with these Central African acquaintances.

But we do know from neurologists who work with babies and patients with brain injuries that non-verbal signals play a major role in social interactions.[4] So, would early populations have needed to understand one another's language to buy and sell from each other? The history of trade shows that language differences did not stop geographically distant people from entering into commerce with each other. Most likely, early communications between speakers of mutually unintelligible languages were through gestures of friendship and peace offerings. In their initial interactions, they would have tried to convey their intentions and emotions through facial expressions, posture, gestures, eye movements and touch. And they would have been able to pick up signs from others too – for example, someone's gaze that may have revealed interest or fear. With continuing contact, particular behavioural patterns would have been reciprocated gradually and evolved into a system for deliberate communication, much like sign languages.

An intriguing idea, which also featured in Herodotus' descriptions, is that of silent trade. According to this (disputed) form of commerce, traders would deposit their goods at a distance from exchange partners, who would then pick these up and leave their own products in return for collection.

> The Carthaginians also tell us that they trade with a race of men who live in a part of Libya beyond the Pillars of Hercules. On reaching this country, they unload their goods, arrange them tidily along the beach, and then, returning to their boats, raise a smoke. Seeing the smoke, the natives come down to the beach, place on the ground a certain quantity of gold in exchange for the goods, and go off again to a distance. The Carthaginians then come ashore and take a look at the gold; and if they think it represents a fair price for their wares, they collect it and go away; if, on the other hand, it seems too little, they go back aboard and wait, and the natives come and add to the gold until they are satisfied. There is perfect honesty on both sides; the Carthaginians never touch the gold until it equals in value what they have offered for sale, and the natives never touch the goods until the gold has been taken away.[5]

However, as markets expanded, verbal language was needed to attract buyers and to be understood by them. Gradually, traders started to adjust to the language of their customers in order to sell; even then, the customer was king.

Trade routes

The most extensive commercial networks for transporting goods in the Old World were waterways. Like Egyptians, many ancient civilizations prospered along their great rivers. They accumulated wealth by selling their crops and manufactured merchandise, whether it was on the Euphrates, the Ganges, the Mekong or the Yellow River. Gradually, improvements in shipping technology made it possible for products to be exchanged over greater distances.

We have archaeological evidence of early long-range trade activities. Bronze Age metal objects retrieved by divers suggest that maritime commercial trade took place between distant ancient civilizations. Finds of seals with inscriptions point to connections as long ago as 3000 BC between civilizations in Mesopotamia (in present day Iraq) and the Harappan society of the Indus Valley (in present day northwestern India and Pakistan).[6] At that time, goods would have passed overland between scattered settlements, and further by water, gradually resulting in trading contacts across this region.

In due course, the cultural exchanges through long-distance trade also kindled a taste for foreign luxury products among the wealthy. Rich people in India and China wanted glassware from Mesopotamia for their houses, others in the Mediterranean fancied textiles, either flax from the Near East or cotton from India. Merchants started to use camel caravans to transport their wares. Since overland trading was slower and more costly than by sea, durable and valuable products were carried to justify the journey. Gradually, such trade took on transcontinental proportions. Among the exotic goods that arrived on the Arabian Peninsula were pearls from Hindustan, ivory from Africa and silk from China. Such commodities were moved up the desert and exchanged in the

Eastern Mediterranean for carpets, metals and ornaments. The travelling merchants were practical people. They worked out that using words from the different languages of their suppliers and middlemen earned them profits. In time, the names of particular goods left their imprints on branches of the commercial networks: among the major transport highways were the Baltic Amber Route and the Oriental Spice and Silk Routes.

By about 200 BC, the Silk Route consisted of an extensive set of maritime and overland passageways connecting the Eastern Mediterranean with Central Asia and China. These commercial arteries eventually extended over 10,000 kilometres. The sea passages led from the Orient to the Persian Gulf or the Red Sea, depending on the season. Then goods were transported overland to the Mediterranean. The main land routes from the West ran from Palmyra in Syria through Babylonia and across northern Iran to the Central Asian oasis city of Merv, from where a southerly route went across Afghanistan to India and a northerly route through vast grassland steppes and arid semi-desert zones north of the Himalayas across Xinjiang to China. Another road came from the caravan city of Petra in the desert between the Red Sea and the Dead Sea to lower Mesopotamia, southern Iran and India. A rich supply of desirable commodities was unloaded, traded or bartered in these commercial hubs, where numerous dealers, entrepreneurs and middlemen from different parts of the world mingled. We know from accounts by traders that Chinese, Persians, Somalis, Greeks, Syrians, Romans, Armenians and Indians were among the many travellers on the road. They brought with them not just their native tongues but also snippets of other languages (perhaps Khotanese, Sogdian or Tibetan) that they had picked up en route. A polyglot community came together on these transcontinental transportation networks.

The steppe was also home to various nomadic tribes (Eurasian nomads or horse people) with their own patchwork of languages that included Uighür and Mongolian. Known for their horsemanship, they have been described as 'fearsome warriors whose lightning-like raids and clouds of arrows terrified their victims'.[7] For them, the story goes, 'raiding and trading were alternate strategies to the same end'. They watched closely the movements of people on the east–west steppe routes leading through terrain that was 'littered with the bleached skeletons of men and beasts'. Both feared and in demand, these nomads are known to have facilitated trade along the way as well as in cities by offering protection from marauding bandits from other migrant tribes. The travelling merchants needed to secure their source of income on these dangerous routes. So they paid the tariffs, which pushed up the cost of overland transport.

With these mutually beneficial measures in place, regular trade and communication between China, Southeast Asia, India, the Middle East, Africa and the Mediterranean soon blossomed. So how did travellers from opposite sides of different continents talk to one another to exchange merchandise, or to ask for directions or help? Speakers of related languages would have used words that were similar. This would have been possible for users of Uighür and Kazakh (which belong to the Turkic family of languages) or of Sogdian and Persian (which are subsets of Iranian). Others would have adopted elements of languages that were more widely understood. For some, this would have been Sogdian, originally spoken in areas around modern Uzbekistan and Tajikistan. This language served as a means of communication on stretches of the Silk Route where the Sogdians were commercially active. An entrepreneurial group of people, they are known to have set up companies with representatives in different cities to facilitate trade, which is probably why their language became widespread. Sogdian merchants also had Chinese protection, which enabled them to extend their commerce (and language) between East and West.

Meanwhile, as we shall see later, what had been happening along the road's western fringes was an early demonstration of the wider phenomenon of languages following power. With growing Hellenic supremacy, a variant of (Koine) Greek started to serve as a language of wider communication in much of the

Mediterranean region. Then, Latin spread with the ascendancy of the Roman Empire. Subsequently, Islamic trade throughout the Middle East brought greater use of Arabic from the seventh century AD onwards. Persian was also spoken in much of the Islamic world, and in time it displaced many other languages, including Sogdian.

Organizing trade

Travel and trade on these interconnecting routes brought people from various cultures together. In the marketplace, dealers and craftsmen met pilgrims, monks, soldiers, nomads and urban dwellers. Not only material artefacts but also knowledge about recent inventions and technological achievements would have been exchanged at these sites. People would have swapped stories about novel ideas such as gunpowder, the compass, printing, paper money or silk making. They would also have discussed their understandings of Judaism, Christianity and Buddhism. Merchants knew that familiarity with their customers' cultures was an important aspect of their trade, as it helped them to build a rapport and more readily negotiate the prices of their goods. Soon the travellers started to settle in trade communities, and learnt the customs and language needed to do business with their hosts. This would then enable them to encourage trade between their adoptive and home societies and to act as agents in the transit of goods. Some of these settlements such as those on the Anatolian peninsula in Asia Minor became centres of literacy and culture with well-organized marketplaces, lodgings and storage facilities; others came and went as the routes changed.[8]

Soon several expansionist powers began to establish maritime commercial bases in other regions to regulate trade and facilitate export. There is evidence of numerous ancient overseas trade settlements on every continent. The Phoenicians colonized the Western Mediterranean, the Egyptians settled in the area now known as Israel, the Greeks established themselves mostly along the Black Sea and around modern Turkey, and the Romans found their base in much of inland Europe. Among the major overseas trade settlements were Carthage (in today's Tunisia), Massalia (later Marseilles), Byzantium (later Constantinople) and Colonia Agrippina (now Cologne). These outposts became economic hubs that connected to other major commercial cities, including Aleppo, Tripoli, Babylon, Damascus, Memphis and Jerusalem. In these socially mixed environments, speakers of different languages mingled. It is easy to imagine how chaos might have ensued with no common means of communication. Foreign merchants would have needed some language support to negotiate their deals, to organize protection from pirates for their return journeys and to order supplies.

In fact, in the early second millennium BC, a solution had already been found in Babylon. Located in Mesopotamia, the fertile basin between the Euphrates and Tigris rivers (largely centred around parts of today's Iraq, Syria and Turkey), this was one of the world's first commercial metropolitan hubs. It bustled with traders and merchants from the Mediterranean, Persia and Turkey, and from beyond India, who came and exchanged goods. In tune with the needs of his time, King Hammurabi[9] exploited his city's growing cultural mix as a resource. He used bilingual foreign traders as cross-cultural brokers. With their language skills, they played a key role in facilitating long-range trade with distant markets. We know this because numerous clay tablets excavated in that region have translations between the lines of text. This is strong evidence that significant portions of the Mesopotamian population were literate in two languages (mostly Sumerian and Akkadian).[10]

Other archaeological finds show that bilingual (possibly even trilingual) scribes mediated between different languages in many other parts of the Old World. The most famous artefact is the Rosetta Stone from the Nile Delta, with parallel texts in ancient Greek and two Egyptian scripts.[11] An older, perhaps less known, example is the inscription on Mount

Behistun in today's Iran, which has three versions of the same text in Old Persian, Elamite and Babylonian. Here, the territories of King Darius[12] are documented, together with advice, blessings and curses, and details of revolts by different tribes.[13] Another bilingual artefact is the Cippi of Melqart in Malta. Two Phoenician marble columns from the second century BC excavated there have engravings in both ancient Greek and Phoenician that led to the modern understanding of the Phoenician language. Then there are the Pyrgi Tablets from the fifth century BC, found in the Italian town of Santa Severa, that record a dedication to a Phoenician goddess. Written in both Etruscan and Phoenician, they led to a clearer understanding of Etruscan.

However, bilingual traders and scribes really provide a solution for communication only within that section of society. What about the rulers of that society? As communities gradually expanded, contact between speakers of different languages became more regular and served more purposes. An ability to use two or more languages to give orders, regulate trade and engage in administration cross-culturally was an advantage. Several early rulers are known to have developed considerable multilingual skills to address their populace and army directly. Pliny the Elder writes that 'Mithridates VI, who was king (during the first century BC in Asia Minor) of twenty-two nations, administered their laws in as many languages, and could harangue in each of them, without employing an interpreter'.[14] Similarly, Cleopatra, reputedly of Greek origin, is said to have learnt several languages:

> She could pass from one language to another; so that there were few of the barbarian nations that she answered by an interpreter; to most of them she spoke herself, as to the Ethiopians, Troglodytes, Hebrews, Arabians, Syrians, Medes, Parthians, and many others, whose language she had learnt; which was all the more surprising because most of the kings, her predecessors, scarcely gave themselves the trouble to acquire the Egyptian tongue.[15]

Knowing Egyptian made Cleopatra popular among her subjects, which enabled her to consolidate her power. Also, learning the languages of her neighbours gave her authority beyond Egypt and brought prosperity to her empire. This was a clever leader who, like Mithridates above, deployed her personal multilingualism strategically as a means to extend her influence.

Recording trade

Expanding trade and governance demanded that written records be kept for everyday transactions and for communication of information. Different systems of writing as expressions of language were employed in the Old World. The use of cuneiform, consisting of wedge-shaped symbols, was widespread for a number of different languages throughout the Middle East. Evidence of transactions in this script dated around 3500 BC comes from Cappadocia in Asia Minor, with excavations that give a record of the commercial operations of an Assyrian trade network. Similarly, among ancient texts found in Mesopotamia are economic accounts written to outline systems of labour and irrigation and to control the administration of goods and the allocation of land. These early scribes would have been remunerated for keeping records, which they wrote with a stylus on tablets of soft clay.

Gradually, lighter writing surfaces (parchment, papyrus or paper) and tools (pen and ink) started to replace heavier materials. This technological revolution facilitated the transportation of written communications across longer distances.[16] Merchants and traders could now produce portable accounts of their commerce, products and routes. But the early scripts had complex symbols in hieroglyphics or cuneiform, which were cumbersome to execute. Commerce demanded an easier method of recording transactions. This became possible by about the tenth century BC, when some Aramaic traders in Western Asia developed a concise writing method: the alphabet.

This relies on a small number of signs that can represent all the words in a language, rather than having a different symbol for each. Because of its ease of use, people gradually started to adopt the alphabet and it spread through maritime trade to North Africa and Europe. Gradually, this system evolved, with some minor adaptations, into the phonetic alphabet used in the West today.

Some two millennia later, another new system would transform the nature of trading: (Hindu-) Arabic numerals. The story goes that travelling traders picked up knowledge about these symbols when buying and selling goods in India. Arab merchants soon adopted their trade partners' method of numeration in their own transactions. By the eighth century AD, people more widely had acquired some familiarity of this system through commercial customs in bazaars and in schools of Western Asia.[17] Numerals allowed merchants to make complex calculations for the conversion of currencies or to determine the price of products such as barrels of wine, sacks of grain and stacks of silk imported from different areas and marked with the weight and measurement units used in their place of origin.

Both these systems of communication, the alphabet and (what we now call) the Arabic numerals, became prevalent because they were more economical and practical to implement than other methods of writing and calculating. Hence, knowledge of them would transfer to many others as economic progress and cultural prosperity grew. Moreover, these imported social practices served imperial organization and the spread of their influence.

Trade and power

One of the economic foundations of empires is trade. To consolidate their powers, many rulers gradually began to assert their authority over particular branches of financially lucrative commercial networks. Some resorted to military means to exert their control, and were in time also using a common language to achieve cultural dominance. One such ruler was Alexander the Great who conquered the Persian Empire in the last decades of the fourth century BC. As a result, Greek culture soon stretched into Central Asia, where it lasted for some three hundred years. The Romans too extended their commercial interests following the conquest of Egypt by Octavian (later called Emperor Augustus) in 30 BC. They are known to have installed Latin-speaking administrators in their trading colonies from Western Europe to Northern Africa and Western Asia. Hence, with the Romans' lasting military and economic superiority, (common, or Vulgar) Latin began to spread across the Mediterranean, merging with other languages.[18]

There was also another – commercial – force that was affecting East–West relationships on trade routes. Wealthy Roman citizens developed a desire for clothing made of silk, which could only be obtained at that time from the Far East. Not only that, this fabric also served as a currency on trade routes. When Emperor Tiberius saw how the demand for this smooth textile was draining his imperial reserves of gold, he issued a trade embargo, banning its purchase. Soon, people wanted to have their own silk. The story goes that, subsequently, in the sixth century AD, Byzantine's Emperor Justinian sent spies from Constantinople to China to steal silkworm eggs with the view of producing this fabric in the West. We know from the historian Procopius that, for this mission, the ruler interviewed monks who had come from India but were actually from Sogdiana.[19] This means that they must have been speakers of an Iranian language. Being educated people, they would also have had some knowledge of Latin or Greek, which were the prevalent languages in the Eastern Roman Empire.

But it is unlikely that they knew Chinese. So how would they have performed their undercover work in China? Would they have used gestures, or a third language or even an interpreter? Their cross-cultural act of (what came to be termed as) early 'industrial espionage' was probably performed successfully since silk started to be manufactured in the West soon afterwards. Whatever the method of communication used, the success of the enterprise illustrates the ingenuity of people when faced with language barriers.

The prosperity that came to the Chinese from trade along the Silk Road was naturally alluring to outsiders. In order to protect their commercial interests, several Chinese emperors used the Great Wall to raise taxes on goods being transported along different parts of the Silk Road.[20] The Chinese also welcomed foreign envoys and merchants in order to forge mutually beneficial commercial ties. These visitors mostly lived in urban centres. We know that in the second half of the first millennium AD, the Tang Dynasty established a Court of Reception to host and interview visiting travellers about their customs, products and places of origin. Records suggest that many of the translators employed for this purpose were drawn from a pool of resident foreigners, predominantly of Inner Asian origin, with some knowledge of spoken Chinese.[21] Their broad knowledge of culture and language would have made them invaluable members of Chinese society.

The power dynamics on the trade routes across Central Asia persisted well into the Middle Ages. In the thirteenth century, the Mongol Empire with Genghis as Khan (or chief) established itself over most of Northern and Central Asia from China to Eastern Europe. This gave new impetus to both trade on the Silk Road network and East–West relationships generally.

Markets and communication

On 24 August 1246 Genghis Khan's grandson Güyük is elected as the new chief in the Mongol capital, Karakorum. Two envoys are present with letters from Pope Innocent IV, in which the Pontiff 'depreciates the massacres and destructions carried out by the Mongols in Europe and requests the King from refraining from further attacks. [The Pope also] hints at a convenient peace treaty'.[22]

The sudden Mongolian advance had caused panic in the West. Who were these Mongols? What were their intentions? The Church warned nations to prepare for a Mongolian invasion. But things turned out quite differently. The whirlwind changes in the East ushered in an era of new opportunities; the Mongols had a history of supporting trade and they welcomed merchants from outside, offering them protection and sanctuary while on the Khans' territories. Under Mongol authority, the commercial routes to the East were open and relatively safe, which resulted in active trade. This made it possible for Westerners to explore new business ventures with partners from different oriental cultures.

Trade and travel

Among the many travellers who made it across Asia were the Polo brothers Niccolò and Maffeo from Venice. Being enterprising merchants, they set out to make a fortune as middlemen for the sale of oriental goods in Europe. They also established trading posts in Constantinople and the Crimea, where the Mongols were present. There, they accepted an invitation to visit Güyük's brother Kubiliai in Dadu (now Beijing), who was the freshly enthroned ruler of China at the eastern end of the Mongolian Empire. In order to control his vast empire, Kubiliai Khan was seeking people who could speak several languages. We know that some of the invited foreigners were even offered posts in the Chinese government. The Khan welcomed the Polo brothers twice, in 1266 and again about a decade later. On this second visit, they brought with them Niccolò's seventeen-year-old son Marco.

Marco Polo subsequently produced a travel record in which he tells us that he held a position of honour at the court, serving as a special envoy to the Khan. His story paints a rich tapestry of the art of trading across cultures in those days. It demonstrates the opportunities opening up in his time through travel and trade. As the envoy in charge of carrying out various diplomatic assignments, Marco provided the Khan with reports from the various places in Asia where he was sent. There is no mention of his needing an interpreter in his communications with Kubiliai, which suggests that he might have known Mongolian. In his own account, he claims that he 'mastered four languages and their modes of writing'[23] but unfortunately provides no further details. Apart from his native Venetian, he may have been able to speak Uighür Turkic and Persian, both of which were used among foreigners working in China. Scholars are unsure as to which would have been his fourth language but think that it was not Chinese since this was not the language of the then rulers. Rather, it could have been Arabic, which he may have learnt earlier in his contacts with Islamic traders in the Middle East.

Marco Polo was certainly interested in languages, and makes numerous references in his account to speech differences between groups of people. One such case is when he mentions that the inhabitants of Kamul (currently Hami City in China's eastern province Xianjiang) 'speak a language of their own'.[24] Writing about the province of Manzi (his term for Southern China), he states that 'one language and one form of writing is current; but there are local differences in speech, as there are … between Lombards, Provençals, Frenchmen etc. but such that [local] people can [nevertheless] understand [one another]'.[25] About the Karajang people in Yunnan, he says that 'they speak a language of their own, which is very difficult to understand'.[26] This suggests that he must have made an effort to pick up some of the local languages as he went along, or at least that he appreciated their divergences.

He had also accumulated knowledge about cultural differences during his outward overland travels and his return voyage by sea. This clearly helped his trade. His 'biographer', widely believed to have been the Romance writer Rusticello da Pisa, saw this as an advantage: 'Messer Marco stayed so long in India, and is so well acquainted with Indian affairs and customs and commerce, that there has scarcely ever been anyone better qualified to give a true account of the country'.[27]

Marco Polo also brought back news about technologies and inventions that he had witnessed from his adoptive base in China. Some of these were hardly known in the West at that time. For example, he knew that pieces of paper of different sizes made from the mulberry tree bark and bearing the imperial seal were used as currency there. With this, he explained, the Khan 'orders all payments to be made ... throughout his empire'. How does the ruler achieve this? Polo has observed that 'no one dares refuse [paper money] on pain of losing his life. All the people ... who are subject to [the Khan's] rule are perfectly willing to accept these papers in payment, since wherever they go they pay in the same currency'.[28] Our narrator must have embraced the customs he encountered, but was likely to have been met with some incredulity regarding these on his return home.

What we have here is a portrait of an able individual who engages himself with people across cultures and learns and uses different languages in so doing. As a foreigner in East Asia, he rises to opportunities and challenges that, simultaneously, make demands on him and extend his skills. He visits countries that few of his contemporaries have seen before and returns over two decades later with fresh insights about new technologies and ways of doing things. He is a modern man in every respect. But Marco did not live to witness the devastating force of change that was about to sweep through the very territories he had visited: the Black Death (or plague).

Trade and change

The Black Death pandemic, which spread to humans through infected fleas carried on rats, is widely believed to have erupted in the Gobi Desert of Mongolia in the mid-fourteenth century. From there, it swept through China, the Near East, Europe and North Africa, killing about a third of the human population. Chroniclers claim that Mongol nomads carried this disease along the overland trade routes to the west, but it may have spread via the sea too. Merchants on the move also caught the plague.[29] One of the accounts on this comes from the Italian notary Gabriele de' Mussi, who heard the following story from sailors: Genoese merchants who travelled to the Black Sea came under siege from the Tartar army in Caffa (now Feodosia, in the Crimea). When the plague broke out, the surviving troops were ordered to hurl their comrades' cadavers from catapults over the city walls. With the rain of the corpses falling, the plague was transmitted to Genoese merchants, who then passed it on to others on their return to Italy.[30]

These apocalyptic events were, in turn, affecting trade practices. Some Italian ports introduced protective measures against the plague and began to turn away vessels suspected of coming from infected areas. Authorities in Venice subjected incoming travellers and legitimate ships to forty days' isolation (hence the term 'quarantine'). Restrictions were also issued on imports and exports, travel and market trading, which resulted in a subsequent reduction in business activity. There now began to be a greater focus on economically profitable direct commercial connections by sea, not only with Asia but also with regions beyond.

As societies gradually recovered from their demographic setback, European rulers wanted to expand their trade and establish commercial bases overseas. They sponsored entrepreneurial explorers to find new passages through the oceans. One of them was Christopher Columbus, formerly a trader along the coasts of West Africa, who journeyed in the 1490s across the Atlantic with support from the Spanish Crown. He was inspired by Marco Polo's adventures and is known to have taken with him an annotated copy of Polo's travel book. Motivated to action by the gold and wealth Columbus brought back to Spain, other ruling powers soon sponsored their own men with promising talents to sail to all continents. This was the start of what came to be called the Age of Discovery.

By now, access to those who could speak multiple languages had become an essential prerequisite, producing a return for merchants and countries. Knowledge of a language used for trade across a relatively large geographic area had particular utility. In the Mediterranean, one approach that was gaining ground to facilitate commerce more widely was the use of a blended language. Infused with (mainly) Italian, French, Spanish, Portuguese, and some Greek, Arabic and Turkish loan words, this adaptable language mixture served as a vehicular means of communication. It enabled merchants to conduct business from their European bases to the North African coastal cities, the Holy Land and the Black Sea. This Mediterranean auxiliary language came to be known as *lingua franca*. In due course, this term was used to designate *any* language drawn on to bridge communication between speakers who do not share a native tongue.

Territory, entrepreneurship, production

The history of trade is studded with accounts of the rise and fall of languages used as lingua francas to facilitate commerce across regions. Occasionally, this could be a language that spread from its initial trade-based origins, such as Phoenician in the Mediterranean or Sogdian in Central Asia. These disappeared with the changing economic conditions. The growing use of Swahili in East Africa, of Arabic across northern Africa and, later, of (Bazaar) Malay in south-east Asia was also influenced by travelling and trading. With imperial expansion from the mid-1500s, other languages (mainly English, French, Italian, Portuguese, Russian and Spanish) began propagating across the globe.

Colonial trade and communication

By the 1500s, the worldview of many Europeans was expanding and so was their desire for goods and raw materials. Within a couple of decades of Columbus' arrival in the 'New World', Vespucci had reached the Brazilian coastline, the Cabots were established in North America and Magellan in the Philippines. Their explorations served the economic interests of monarchies that sought to establish commercial connections with new overseas regions. The European colonial era had begun, and over the next four hundred years, various imperial powers would hoist their flags in territories that were prized for their resources as well as climate and geographic positions. The Portuguese started early (in 1557), when China allowed them to use a maritime trading post in Macau. Apparently, this favour was in return for services rendered to the Chinese in clearing their pirate-infested seas. They also installed themselves in Latin America, as did the Spanish. Soon, other Europeans followed, securing overseas indigenous resources for export. By the mid-eighteenth century, the 'New World' was divided up between Britain, France and also Spain; meanwhile, many European powers were setting up bases in Africa.

The ever-increasing range of new raw materials that began to reach Europe's growing industrial economy was satisfying people's appetites for fresh types of manufactured products and consumables. Already by the closing decades of the seventeenth century, the demand for imported textiles (mainly silk and cotton) and consumables (tea, coffee, sugar and tobacco) had increased dramatically in Western Europe. There is evidence from household inventory studies in the Netherlands and England that not only the rich but also people at large wanted these luxury goods.[31] This was a huge boost to colonial trade, which now delivered greater quantities of commodities, opening up an early form of global capitalism. But this practice also entailed unequal relationships that were sustained by communication barriers between the various imperial and local negotiators who often had no language in common.

For practical purposes, indigenous peoples soon started to develop makeshift jargons. These vehicular tools of communication, described as consisting of 'choppy strings of words borrowed from the language of the colonizers or plantation owners … with no consistent rules', became known as 'pidgins'.[32] A bit like the Mediterranean lingua franca, these manufactured jargons came into circulation through extended and regular trade contact. They served the locals as a basic means of interaction with officials, merchants, sailors and other representatives of power. Gradually, as the colonial powers established numerous labour intensive economies throughout the world, pidgins became associated with trade, agriculture and mining. But these were restricted speech forms and, hence, had a low prestige with respect to other languages. Many of them have since died out; others evolved over the course of several generations into more complex, native languages, now known as 'creoles'. This happened where communities of speakers stayed together over long periods of time, for example as slave labourers on tobacco, rice or cotton plantations. Some creoles became widespread, as in the case of Swahili, which was used along trading and slave routes in eastern Africa. Numerous other creoles are still spoken today, in the Caribbean, Papua New Guinea, West Africa and Australia. Both pidgins and creoles flourished worldwide with the expansion of trade and power.[33]

Many of Europe's imperial languages have left a lasting impression in numerous zones of the world. To various degrees, they still are a feature in many regions – from the Americas to parts of Africa, Asia and Oceania. The actual extent of penetration of these exported languages in the various territories depended on the nature of the contact established there. English, for example, diffused more in countries where the colonizers settled (America, Australia, Canada) than in regions of resource extraction (Malaysia, Nigeria). The term 'linguistic imperialism' was coined to describe the practice of using imperial languages in colonial territories.[34] This view links political dominance and economic exploitation with language dominance and asymmetric exchange. We shall see later how in due course numerous economically less viable indigenous languages were displaced, replaced or supplemented by languages with a greater reach and, hence, greater power.

Language and territory

It is easy to see how the growing economic and military reach of imperial rulers crystallized into ideas of territoriality, both materially and culturally. This expansion propelled a profound social transformation and changed political structures. As some royal dynasties, for example the Bourbons in France or the Ottomans in Turkey, were centralizing power and governing through bureaucracies in the language of the court they also forged a closer association between language and territory.

From the sixteenth century onwards, another development that promoted this connection was the growth of the printing business. Johannes Gutenberg's more elaborate printing technology[35] meant that manuscripts could now be mass-produced at relatively affordable costs. A landmark publication was Martin Luther's translation of the New Testament from Koine Greek to German. This appeared in 1522, and his complete Bible followed twelve years later. While this was not the first published Bible, it had a widespread circulation that also facilitated the emergence of a standard, modern German that speakers of the many diffuse dialects used at that time could understand. Similarly, the translation of the Bible into Welsh by William Morgan in 1588 is widely thought to have played a role in the survival of the Welsh language.

Gradually, as printers set up business in Rome, Venice and Paris, they began to cater for a new urban class. Their trade was linked with economic and technological developments in other branches of industry and commerce, which led to a search for new means to boost productivity. The printers used fewer print languages and invested in machinery that shortened book production time, leading to greater profits. With increasing literacy rates among speakers of these languages, the market for printed material duly expanded. Substantial print runs were now needed for widened circulation of published texts to satisfy demand by larger readerships. By the nineteenth century, these developments went alongside a growing sense of national identity in Europe, which was further consolidated through modernization and industrialization. Over time, trade and industry became inextricably linked with national cultures and the languages that were now used for state governance.[36]

But this alignment of nationalism, capitalism and technology adversely affected linguistic diversity as people started to adopt their country's official language, often by coercion. For example, speakers of Galician began to shift to Spanish, speakers of Breton to French and those of West Frisian to Dutch. Moreover, the gradual move to societal monolingualism meant that smaller language communities became marginalized. A language-centric approach has more or less been adopted by every newly emergent independent country since the decline of the era of colonialism after the Second World War, and also subsequently, by many post-Soviet states. As the recent events in the Balkans demonstrated, this language-based national ideal is still in vogue today, with Serbo-Croatian splitting into Serbian, Croatian and Bosnian.

Today, the majority of the world's almost two hundred independent countries have formally chosen the monolingual route. Around the globe, English is most prominently featured as a state language, followed by French, Arabic, Spanish and Portuguese. Yet, a homogeneous take on societal language usage hardly corresponds with what people really speak on the ground. An estimated 6,000–7,000 languages are in existence around the world today (depending on whether you consider certain languages to be dialects or vice versa). This means that multilingualism is extremely common – the rule rather than the exception.

Modern-day attitudes often embrace cultural diversity, for example, in terms of languages spoken, clothes worn and religion followed. But there is also a need for its economic consequences to be recognized. In today's world, with its fast social, cultural and material changes, the challenge lies in keeping up the momentum of innovatively embracing language diversity to meet societal and market needs. Officially adopting more than one language at state level would be a major step towards supporting language heterogeneity. Among the many countries that formally recognize several languages are Singapore (4), Senegal (7) and South Africa (11). But is this approach enough? In other words, how can multilingualism be exploited innovatively as a resource to promote social well-being and economic growth?

Demand, supply, resources

The previous sections have shown how since earliest times people have used languages in innovative ways. We have seen how merchants, colonizers and rulers deployed their own or other languages strategically to do business, obtain resources and extend their powers. Overall, employment of particular languages other than their own often served their commerce, industry and national politics.

So, clearly, languages can propel business. What is perhaps not so obvious is that business can propel languages. Let's use an analogy. Take the example of the rare earth metals (yttrium, terbium and europium, among others). Sixty years ago, these elements mostly lay buried deep in the ground. Yet, now, they are vital in the manufacture of semiconductors used in electronics. They are essential ingredients for hundreds of applications we take for granted nowadays, from mobile phones to laptops, jet engines and medical imaging. These elements are also critical for transition to a renewable energy economy, as they are needed to manufacture products such as solar cells and wind turbines. In brief, our twenty-first century hi-tech lifestyle would not be the same without the use of rare earth metals.[37]

In a similar way, as recently as the 1990s, Mandarin Chinese was viewed as a specialty in the Western world; it had few learners and was taught in just a few schools; hardly any university offered courses in the language. Yet, the rising economic power of China has propelled the use of Mandarin Chinese and its promotion in education to the point that nowadays it is perceived by many politicians and educationalists as *the* language to learn. For instance in 2007, just 7.8 per cent of the UK's state schools offered Mandarin. Now, 17 per cent do so, with 45 per cent of independent schools featuring the language.[38] The economic power of China has driven the growth of Mandarin Chinese.

But is this situation stable, or sustainable? The changing winds of the free market are opening up rare earth mineral production in other regions of the world, away from China. From Australia to Vietnam, Malaysia and Brazil, countries are positioning themselves to extract rare earths. In similar ways, with the continuing demand for the export of raw materials and the import of technology, skilled individuals from across the world will be sought for employment in management, construction, assembly, processing, engineering and, of course, in the negotiation of contracts. Many of them will need to be able to speak Vietnamese, Malay or Portuguese. So, our demand for globalized products can influence the flows of capital, goods, people and languages in most unexpected ways.

What should individuals from outside these language regions do if they want to share in this prosperity? Faced with this economic reality, do they rely on translation or choose to learn one of the languages of these growing powers? And if so, which ones and for what purpose? Soon the Chinese economy may be the largest in the world. With Western entrepreneurs responding to this incentive, the market value of Mandarin Chinese has risen and younger generations are being trained to realize its economic potential. But how can we be sure that the Chinese economy will continue to grow? Just how many Mandarin-speaking Westerners will be required by 2030, or 2050?

However, the long time lag between learning and using any language means that prediction of language demand will always be difficult, if not impossible. For language acquisition planning, this could mean that particular curricular choices may eventually not match the changing language needs as generated by the vagaries of the market. Or governments may acknowledge that a certain language can benefit trade, but they may not be prepared to invest in it for the long term, through education. In addition, individuals who do decide to learn a particular language may give it up or opt not to use it, so the societal benefit of individual language choices is difficult to gauge.

Others who persist with their study will in many ways do so to get on in life, whether professionally or personally. But whether someone benefits materially from knowing another language depends on market forces that are outside an individual's control. To be successful, our decisions need to be based on an informed understanding of the market potential of multilingualism. In our aspirations for individual and societal growth, we require insight into how multilingual skills interconnect with the globalizing economy, employment and social cohesion. The questions to consider are the following: What is the market value of languages? How is language traded? Does it have a price? What is the service that is the subject of market forces?

CHAPTER TWO

Economic aspects of languages today

This chapter considers the link between economics and language policy. When official decisions are made about language use in a country, region or organization, it results in a language policy. These policies can have different and complementary aims – for example, governments may formally promote one or several languages. Thus, Finland supports two official languages (Finnish and Swedish) and also Sami, which is spoken by indigenous people in its Arctic region. Nevertheless, Finnish is the country's predominant language. In order to work, such measures need to be economically sustainable and supported by an appropriate education policy. Several language interventions may be made successively to change public language use in a given country. In Belgium, a series of state reforms were set in motion to accommodate the language demands of its French-, Dutch- and German-speaking communities. Most language policies require finance for implementation and, as a result, decisions are often made on the basis of cost–benefit calculations. Perhaps surprisingly, little work has been carried out on the effects of such policies, despite the fact that any government decision about language, including simply maintaining the status quo, can have profound economic consequences.

To try and understand the economic aspects of language policymaking today, we can look to Canada and, in particular, to the French-speaking province of Quebec, in order to examine the impact of a public language decision made there nearly forty years ago. The new regulations were designed 'to make French the language of Government and the Law, as well as the normal and everyday language of work, instruction, communication, commerce and business'.[1] Despite meeting opposition, the reforms are continuing. A recent headline from CBC News Montreal warned: 'Quebec to tighten language law, force retailers to add French descriptions to names.'[2] The accompanying article outlined the latest measures that the Quebec government was planning 'to oblige major retailers to include French wording in their commercial English signage'. Some of the Quebec companies responded to the language watchdog's order by combining English with French as in 'Les Magasins Best Buy'. Others such as Wal-Mart are keen to maintain their right to keep their original (English) name intact.

The switch to French introduced in 1977 aimed not only to safeguard the language in Quebec but also to support the economic opportunities of French Canadians. To do business,[3] local and foreign companies selling products or services in Quebec must follow set language requirements. Employers have to use French in written documents meant for their staff and customers. French is also expected to be used for product labelling, public signs and commercial advertising, including websites. All businesses have to be able to serve the public in French. Therefore, every job applicant must have French language ability. However, at the same time, in Quebec, employees need a basic knowledge of English to enable them to serve non-French-speaking customers.

Clearly such changes required enormous political will, did not come cheaply and were even socially divisive. What has meanwhile been learnt and have the changes achieved their intended aims?

Calculating language choices

While the Francization policy in Quebec has produced noticeable gains for individuals and society alike, it has been costly. The outlay included the work of government agencies to implement the objectives (approximately C$20 million per annum), language training for civil servants (around C$5.5 billion per annum) and translation of official documents (C$90 million per annum).[4] There were further costs during the first five years of the switch to French. It has been estimated that 0.2 per cent of the provincial output and 2 per cent of employment were lost. This change also added to business expenditures and resulted in an exodus of head offices and the loss of business confidence.[5]

It is natural to ask whether this effort was worth it and whether the objectives of the various programmes were met. On the basis of available figures of public outgoings, the Canadian economist François Vaillancourt conducted a cost–benefit analysis of these measures.[6] His calculations focused on both running costs and anticipated returns on service investments. He showed that the economic cost was less than 0.5 per cent of the province's GDP. While admitting that the overall outlay was high, he concluded that it was relatively low in view of the achieved outcomes in enabling improved competitiveness of the French language and its speakers in Canadian society. For example, although English speakers still tend to make more money than French speakers (perhaps because they have more earning potential beyond Quebec), the income gap between these two groups has dramatically decreased since the 1970s. In particular, in the public sector (where French must be used), Francophones enjoy a wage premium. Other commentators have suggested that improvements have occurred for the population as a whole in terms of social justice, education and earning opportunities, especially when considering average earnings, language ability and cross-cultural communication.[7] An unexpected outcome has been that Francization appears to have led to greater societal multilingualism in the province rather than just an increase in the use of French.

The level of material investment appears to have been sustainable because the overall situation of the French language in Quebec has remained healthy over the period in question. Nevertheless, this may change in the future as a result of the low birth rate and the fact that many migrants to Canada choose the more predominant language (English). This reflects a global trend where people tend to move to the language of the more powerful economy. Not surprisingly, newcomers to Quebec are offered French language courses free of charge.

The Francization policy seems to have been justified over time at the societal level. Its effects on individuals have been considered as part of research on the socio-economic status in Quebec. According to the 2011 Census, over a million people in the rest of Canada, living in provinces with no such policy (mainly New Brunswick and Ontario), speak French as their first language. Recent studies on connections between second language skills and earnings differentials identified higher rates for French-English bilingualism in Quebec than in other parts of Canada.[8] So it would seem that someone who is bilingual is better off in a region where that bilingualism is officially supported.

In Europe, language policies of a different kind have been in existence for a long time. A prime example is Switzerland, which has four territorial languages that have been officially adopted by its twenty-six cantons in different ways (Grisons is trilingual; Berne, Fribourg and Valais are all bilingual; the others are monolingual). Many of the country's citizens are also proficient in English. The Swiss economist François Grin carried out a survey[9] that showed regional preferences for second language skills. While higher wage differentials were noted everywhere for proficiency in English, this was greater in German-speaking Switzerland than in the French- or Italian-speaking parts. In the latter two regions, knowledge of German is rewarded even more highly than of English. This shows that bilingualism with a second national language tends to yield greater returns when this community is economically stronger. Thus English has more economic value for someone in German-speaking Zurich, and German for someone in Italian-speaking Lugano.

Other work on language-related earnings confirmed that advantages are often language specific. In 2005, the urban economist Albert Saiz based at the Massachusetts Institute of Technology (MIT) carried out a study on direct benefits of language skills for US graduates.[10] He showed that proficiency in Spanish brought just a 1.7 per cent wage premium, as opposed to an average income boost of 2.7 per cent for French and 4 per cent for Mandarin, German, Italian and Russian. He links the difference to the law of supply and demand. There is a sizeable Hispanic population in the United States able to offer Spanish, which may explain why graduates in that language find themselves caught up in a market that is saturated. Conversely, in the relative absence of native speakers of Mandarin, German, Italian and Russian, the demand for people skilled in these languages is greater.

By showing correlations between particular language skills and earnings differentials in different regions, these empirical findings from Quebec, Switzerland and the United States can have profound implications both for individuals when it comes to choosing which language to learn and for language education policymaking at the local, regional and national levels.[11] They suggest that regional assessments are essential to determine the appropriate amount of investment required for language curricula and training. At the same time, it is hard to escape the conclusion that if a language policy takes the blanket approach of monolingual practice, it may well fail to deliver economic benefits.

The focus on language-related earnings can also extend to migration. Linking language proficiency with human capital development, a study by economists Hoyt Bleakley and Aimee Chin showed that income gains of English-speaking immigrants to the United States were on average 30 per cent higher compared to those of their non-English-speaking cohorts.[12] Complementary findings from a series of cross-national investigations in the United States, Israel, Canada and Australia carried out by the Washington-based economist Barry Chiswick also point to economic benefits for immigrant groups with destination language skills.[13] In particular, he showed that, apart from the financial return that flows from an individual's ability to function in the language of the host economy, this also has a significant pay-off in terms of promoting social adjustment and civic participation. This empirical work suggests that countries can expect economic gains if they provide language training for newcomers.

An economics perspective

The language policies in Quebec initiated a range of studies that systematically examined the links between language and economics. Much of this research has considered the language behaviour of individuals as related to earnings differentials. The main thrust was to view second language skills as a form of 'human capital' in which people and societies invest. For individuals learning another language, this implies using personal resources in anticipation of future benefits. For governments and businesses, supporting forms of language training can be seen as a means of obtaining an economic advantage.

But what about finding the resources to implement such policies, even if the political will is there? This question is relevant not only at the national or regional level, but also within companies and for individuals. Economic models need to take account of the allocation of 'scarce' resources among competing ends to be able to assist policy matters. 'Scarcity' implies that the resources are limited and that something must be given up to acquire them, such as spending time or money to manage multilingual communication in an organization. Moreover, time used in one activity cannot usually be spent on another activity. This means that choices need to be made.

For example, when a Syrian refugee newly arrives in Quebec, she will consider whether to learn French or English (she may not have the time or energy to study both at the same time). On the one hand, French would open up doors to the labour market in the province, but this choice might mean that she would have to learn English if she wanted to find employment elsewhere in Canada. On the other hand, mastery of English alone would be restrictive in Quebec but could make a future move to the rest of Canada easier. By selecting one language option she may miss out on benefits from the other at some future time. She has to pay the opportunity cost of her decision, which has to be weighed against the actual benefits she will get from the choice made.

However, sometimes a focus on the material return on investment (ROI) of developing proficiency in a particular language is not relevant. In fact, many language-related decisions are not done on cost–benefit grounds alone, but can also involve other, less tangible considerations. The move above to Quebec may actually be socially motivated, perhaps to join family there. In terms of expected benefits, this prospect might well outweigh the appeal of securing employment more widely in Canada. In such cases, the costs of a decision are difficult to estimate, just as the expected benefits are also elusive.

There are different views in economics on how to include the vagaries of human behaviour. According to one school of thought, humans, being in possession of all the facts necessary to make a decision, act rationally and in a selfish way to get what they want. This suggests that we wisely use the limited resources available to us in selecting the best possible course of action to satisfy our needs. Assuming we proceed logically on the basis of our accumulated knowledge, we settle on a choice that maximizes the benefits we hope to get, whether materially or otherwise. But there are times when a language decision we make might appear non-optimal in material terms. Such a choice may have overriding emotional, cultural or political significance to us.

So, a language is not a widget that can be manufactured, bought or sold with no other value attached to it. A distinction is made in economics between the market (or direct) value of products or services as reflected in costs, prices and wages and the non-market (or indirect) value that is more difficult to capture in figures. For example, the measurable value of multilingualism covers costs (of providing services), wages (for someone with language skills) and price (of producing signage in multiple languages). Less tangible values include other aspects of social life such as culture, identity and human rights. When it comes to personal language learning preferences, both direct and indirect values may play a role. For example, our Syrian refugee above may in her language choice weigh up both the expected material gains (of widened employment prospects through knowledge of English) and less tangible social benefits (of sharing her family members' adopted culture). She might decide to learn French, reasoning that 'not everything that counts can be counted'[14] in material terms.

The studies in Quebec, Switzerland, the United States and elsewhere show how an economics perspective can be adopted to compare and evaluate the cost-effectiveness of language choice options. This information can be useful when making decisions about language policy measures in education, for language service provision and particular language interventions in a range of other social settings. Assessing the effect of language skills on income and trade may also serve individuals in making informed language choices. But from our efforts to judiciously use the limited resources available, we also know that some important things in social life are not measurable.

Modelling multilingualism

The above examples are not unique. Nowadays, globalization and the Internet have brought more people into contact with more languages than ever before. This greater prominence of multilingualism in many Western societies is widely recognized. But how can this language mix be dealt with? Should we all learn many languages? Should all public announcements be made in several languages? Or should, perhaps, everyone speak English? Securing public and private investments for the provision of language services in language-diverse settings can represent a major challenge, not only politically but also economically. Consequently, there is now a greater focus on the economics of multilingualism. The empirical studies on the economic benefits and drawbacks of specific language policy decisions discussed above have used publicly available data. Other work has tried to model the budgetary implications of multilingualism in countries, international organizations and companies.

A macro-economic approach

A Canadian–Swiss collaboration has looked at the economic benefit of multilingualism in society.[15] The model they used assumes that costs and benefits rise along with the growth of multilingualism. Their findings suggest that a monolingual society that becomes bilingual could derive benefits.[16] But the model also showed that beyond a certain level, increasing multilingualism leads to costs that exceed benefits. For example, adding one language introduces more translation costs that rise in direct proportion to the number of languages used. However, the benefits of that extra language may only be felt at the margins. This implies that there is an optimal number of languages an organization or a country can support in practice. To determine this, a full analysis of the economic performance would be necessary in each case.

A more sophisticated model was subsequently developed that linked language variables with economic variables. Language variables include the number of languages involved, the existing language skills and the amount of time it takes to learn another language. Economic variables cover GDP, the unemployment rate, the inflation rate, the interest rate, the level of the stock market and exchange rates.[17] In the case of Switzerland, the economic value of multilingualism was estimated to be 9 per cent of its GDP.[18] Hence, multilingualism can be considered a source of considerable wealth for the country. In particular, the value of multilingualism to IT services has been calculated to be nearly 25 per cent and its value to the chemical, transport and mechanical engineering industries to be over 15 per cent each. In their comprehensive analysis, the researchers suggest that the way a society values its multilingualism affects the public and private investment options chosen and, in turn, the social and economic outcomes.

Such quantitative models can provide quite detailed results. But they are often cumbersome and contain a number of assumptions that are most likely country-specific. There have also been qualitative studies carried out at the micro-economic level to analyse the effects of multilingual capabilities on business. The British Chambers of Commerce found a direct correlation between annual turnover and the value managers placed on language skills.[19] Findings show that linguistic and cultural barriers led to loss of contacts, turnover and profitability and also to a reluctance to tackle new markets. These observations come on top of evidence from an earlier European Commission survey of nearly 2,000 businesses, which found that 11 per cent of respondents had lost a contract as a result of a lack of language skills. At least ten of these contracts were worth over €1 million each.[20]

So, on the one hand (macro-economically), we have a detailed economic study showing that in one multilingual country (Switzerland), multilingualism can have a strong positive benefit. Then, on the other hand (micro-economically), we have hard evidence that individual monolingualism can harm business performance. Put together, these findings make a strong economic case for language learning. Yet, in many countries, particularly in the English-speaking world, foreign language learning budgets are kept low, for both formal education and vocational training. Hence, education policy makers in such regions tend to emphasize language utility when arguing for more resources. Frequently, their recommendations are influenced by economic forecasts that predict gains to be made from learning particular languages. But a purely market-driven approach can cloud a more subtle analysis, namely that, within optimal limits, unregulated individual multilingualism may also lead to economic gains.

Communication in international organizations

The management of language use in large international organizations also has economic implications. Essentially, the choice revolves around using a global language as the lingua franca, resorting to translating and interpreting or a combination of both approaches. The United Nations (UN) and the World Trade Organization (WTO) exhibit complex multilingual structures. This means that decisions have to be made about which languages to use for working relationships. But the practicalities of securing effective internal communication in accordance with the changing participation dynamics are challenging. For example, six languages are used in United Nations meetings and for the dissemination of its official documents: Arabic, English, French, Mandarin, Russian and Spanish. The World Trade Organization uses a 'leaner' approach, with English, French and Spanish as its working languages. These two organizations selected a small set of languages in which to conduct their business, an approach that could be considered optimal. At another major international organization, an essentially monolingual approach was adopted: for the World Bank, the main medium of communication is English, with conferences also offering simultaneous interpreting into Arabic, Mandarin, French, Russian and Spanish. Then, at the other end of the spectrum, the European Union operates in three core languages (mainly English, with French and German) and also has responsive policies to serve the remaining official language groups of its member states. It is regarded as one of the world's most highly dynamic organizations in terms of the multiplicity of languages used within its institutions.

This range of official and working languages used for internal communication in international organizations may change with the joining of additional members. In the European Union, for example, the number of languages used has grown from four in 1958 (the languages of the founding member states were Dutch, French, German and Italian) to twenty-four official languages used in twenty-eight member states by 2015. This means that the number of languages used in the European Union's institutions has expanded sixfold since its inception just over half a century ago. The management of this language diversity is a contentious issue, not only in terms of (direct) costs to the taxpayer, but also in terms of its effectiveness and fairness in ensuring democratic participation. Could this vast language apparatus with its dependence on translation and interpreting services be streamlined with a universal language? This is already being practised to some extent. We know, for example, that in the United Nations and the European Union, some documents are made available solely in English, with a few in some additional languages, depending on the context. The possible benefits of deploying a universal language are sometimes discussed, but a monolingual regime has not (yet) been systematically introduced in major international organizations with a multilingual structure, although the World Bank comes close.

Economic considerations have featured in a recent investigation on ways to manage multilingual communication in the European Union's institutions.[21] Two alternative language regime scenarios (translation and interpreting *versus* introducing English as the universal language of communication) were evaluated in terms of costs and criteria of effectiveness and fairness. The latter approach relies on the learning of one language by all non-native speakers. The former requires less language acquisition but consistent use of translation and interpreting. Findings point to a multilingual, translation-based language regime as being more effective than a unilingual regime based on English. With an estimated annual expenditure of approximately €2.50 per EU citizen,[22] translation and interpreting, the researchers propose, are economically sustainable. The suggestion was also made that this approach may be fairer in fostering democratic participation. So here we have the beginnings of an approach where both material costs and non-market values are included in the assessment of a language policy.

With the increasing remit and power of international organizations, both the volume and the need for translation are set to grow dramatically. Currently, in the European Union, the verbal communications in meetings are translated into twenty-four languages. Hence language services have to deal with 552 individual acts of interpreting (or 276 language pairs) every time they are deployed. This means that future investment in translation will need to keep up with further expansion. For example, the possible admission of Turkey into the European Union would require an additional twenty-four language-pair translations. So, economic considerations will doubtless become more central in informing multilayered and ever-evolving organizational language regime policy while also needing to ensure effective verbal exchanges. Clearly, there is no template for dealing with multilingualism in language-diverse settings. But investment in flexible multilingual solutions would seem to make economic sense to bridge gaps in communication.

Language policy and profit

As in the case of existing international organizations, new multilingual needs will be important in a range of emerging trade blocs around the world. The four big BRIC countries of

Brazil, Russia, India and China have fast-growing economies and they are in discussion with Mexico and South Korea as possible additional members. Other clusters include CIVETS (Columbia, Indonesia, Vietnam, Egypt, Turkey, South Africa) and EAGLEs, which is a more dynamic concept based on anticipated growth in a wider range of economies. While these loose groupings may not develop into a trade bloc in the same way as the European Union, or the ASEAN (Association of Southeast Asian Nations) have, these developments suggest that the global marketplace is fluid and also becoming more interconnected.

The likely greater interaction of countries within and between these clusters will produce complex language dynamics revolving chiefly around those of the more major players. For example, the 'R' of BRIC (Russia) will also cultivate trade relations with other growing Eastern European economies, namely the Baltic countries, Bulgaria, the Czech Republic, Hungary, Poland, Romania and Slovakia, probably with interactions mainly carried out in Russian. Companies that operate in any part of these clusters will need a clear language policy to meet the demands this will make. As is further discussed in Chapter 5, fluency in English is limited in some of these emerging economies relative to their rising purchasing power. Therefore, any multinational corporation seeking to penetrate these markets will need to focus on the languages that are used there, besides English.

Without a strategic corporate language policy, trade relations and export performance can suffer. A recent survey carried out by the *Economist*[23] gives evidence of losses incurred by large companies that did not pay sufficient attention to corporate language matters. The widely acknowledged communication barriers in different industries occasionally serve as an argument for more language education. Arguably, such investment would be justified on the grounds that effective multilingual communication enhances international competitiveness. A case could be made for government-sponsored schemes, perhaps in the form of tax breaks, to complement organizational support of internal language training. Such funding would likely be responsive to changes in the market but could also help foster greater commercial productivity for overall national economic gain.

An interim strategic approach for reaching out to new markets is through selected intermediary languages, for example Spanish across Latin America, and Russian in Eastern Europe. But the use of fewer languages may lead to reduced opportunities in export services as potential openings might be missed or overlooked. Moreover, some consumers are unwilling or unable to respond to such a blanket approach in marketing, preferring, instead, to choose their goods by comparing different suppliers.

The challenge of providing widening target groups with export products in their primary language is nowadays often met with outsourcing. This has led to a rapid expansion of the language services industry where language skills are bought and sold. In these language-intensive markets, the economic value of language skills is naturally high, as in the information and communication technology (ICT) industry. Chapter 5 discusses how this commodification of languages serves to generate profit.

Balancing language choices

We return, then, to Canada. As we have seen, Quebec's language policy was introduced chiefly in order to safeguard its French language setting and also to improve the wealth of francophone Quebecers. The first of these reasons, which would appear to have no direct market benefits, is culturally motivated. It derives from the history of this province and from contemporary concerns that English was going to overwhelm French. The second reason is clearly economic in character.[24]

Similar considerations can also be seen in the language choices of our Syrian refugee on her move to Canada. Forced to leave her native country and in search of employment, she decides to join her French-speaking relatives in Quebec. But once there, she may eventually also learn English and end up as functionally trilingual. Each of these choices would have involved a combination of economic and cultural considerations: the rational meeting the emotional.

We can observe similar behaviours operating at many different levels of society and also in organizations. The United Nations, for example, contains members that represent hundreds of languages spoken in the world. Yet, the organization operates officially with just six languages. This would appear to be a decision that places operational functionality ahead of democratic representation. Do the other cultures feel marginalized because their language is not represented? Or, if they were all included, would the United Nations cease to function? On the other hand, the European Union operates with a plethora of languages. Everyone is, at least formally, on an equal footing. But are monetary resources being wasted to allay democratic concerns? Then we have the World Bank, with its essentially monolingual approach. Certainly business is likely to run smoothly this way, but what cultural benefits are being missed as a result?

And then at the national level, we see a host of different policies being used. At one end of the scale are the United States and Australia who, despite their language-rich immigrant settings, have officially chosen the monolingual route. Could their latent language resources be activated for economic gain? Findings from a recent report show that the US federal government alone has spent US$ 4.5 billion on outsourced language services over two decades since 1990.[25] A language skills deficiency results in a lucrative business for some but can represent a huge loss for others. Could countries in general benefit from releasing their largely dormant language resources by embracing them more overtly? One such model is devolution, which has earned economic benefits since the 1980s for Spain's autonomous language regions Catalonia, Galicia and the Basque Country, as also, since the 1990s, for

Wales in the UK. At the other end of the scale are countries such as Switzerland, where the economic gains of official multilingualism have already been ascertained.

Language policy in companies is considered in greater detail in the next chapters. But, again, we will see how the balance of choices weighs on any decision. To go multilingual requires effort and may not be cheap, but the opportunity costs of multilingualism can be considerable. In this instance, the benefits of using more than one language are initially related to tapping into the cultural backgrounds of employees, who then contribute more to the profitability of their organization.

The lack of assessment of the economic relevance of language policy at any level of society is a real issue. Little research has been carried out in this area, while cuts are being made to language education budgets. At the same time, there is plenty of evidence for how an adherence to purely economic motives is leading to the extinction of many lesser-used languages. Language ecologies are being washed away by an economic tsunami, just as biodiversity is threatened by monocultures in agriculture.

Language diversity economics

A major theme in this book is that languages follow power, whether politically, economically or through personal ambition. Adopting a stronger language enables people to join larger communities of communication and, hence, to access more opportunities. The main forces causing language shift nowadays are globalization as well as the monolingual national ideal. These homogenizing drives have caused the decline, and even loss, of numerous smaller languages across the globe.

Illustrating this trend is the headline 'Economic success drives language extinction', which recently featured on the BBC website.[26] The background to this news item was a study in which an international group of scientists set out to elicit why and where many of the world's languages are being lost. They observed that high economic growth is among the socio-economic factors that affect languages at risk.[27] In particular, they showed that recent small-language-speaker declines are strongly linked to a rising GDP income per capita, especially in regions of high latitudes. The researchers forecast that language-rich territories undergoing rapid economic growth, for example in the tropics and in the Himalayas, will be the primary areas of small-language losses in the near future. They call for conservation efforts to focus on these parts of the world.

More widely, in regions from Papua New Guinea to Indonesia, Kenya and the Amazon, economic realities mean that cultural ecologies are threatened when foreign-based corporations move in to extract commodities or establish monoculture plantations. Furthermore, across the Himalayas, major dam projects are affecting fragile language habitats in Pakistan, India, Bhutan and Nepal. In these countries, the shift of people to a more dominant language is motivated by their need to build sustainable livelihoods. Migration to cities for work further accelerates this trend, causing individuals to abandon their mother tongues. Without protective national policies, many affected indigenous language ecologies are draining away. This can be observed all over the world, from Australia to Africa and Canada. Such dying languages are usually those spoken by relatively powerless peoples. No powerful ethnic or cultural grouping loses its language.[28]

These developments illustrate the undeniable challenge for small-language regions posed by globalization. Numerous schemes have been launched to halt or reverse the decline of language ecologies. Successful attempts from different continents include Maori in New Zealand, Sami in Northern Scandinavia and Ainu in Northern Japan. There is a saying that 'a language you do not teach, you kill'. This means that schools can play a central role in the revival of threatened languages by encouraging their use either as a medium of instruction or as a subject of study. Revitalization initiatives can make a real difference when carried out in concert with other social organizations to create incentives and opportunities for speakers to use their language in the economic sphere too.

Through entrepreneurial activities, local empowerment is likely to be more pervasive. A new generation of speakers for whom this has worked, among others, are users of Welsh in Wales or of Catalan in Catalonia. Most prominently, the 1992 Summer Olympics in Barcelona brought lasting economic and cultural benefits, generating inputs for both urban and cultural renewal through the Catalan language. With the possibility of improved economic returns in the shape of employment or other gains, the political will and grassroots support for revival efforts are likely to be stronger. But such endeavours are not without controversy, as they also risk being perceived as a barrier by outsiders.

Moreover, minority languages often suffer an image problem. It is sometimes assumed that they have limited usefulness or are backward, which partly accounts for speaker losses. Naturally, a language that has appeal in the eyes of the community of its users has a greater chance of survival. Websites, YouTube and social media can serve as a means to draw in people more widely. An example was the recent YouTube video of fourteen-year-old Peruvian Renata Flores Rivera singing Michael Jackson's 'The Way You Make Me Feel' in Quechua, an indigenous language of South America, once used by the Incas.[29] This video was made as part of a project called 'Las juventudes tambien hablamos Quechua' ('The youth, we speak Quechua too'). Quechua-speaking Peruvians (who make up about one-fifth of the country's total population) are experiencing an existential challenge. To be able to function in their country, they need to learn Spanish, the language of commerce, education and government. But for some time now, they have been pushing for the maintenance and preservation of their language, including the right of Quechua-speaking children to be taught in their mother tongue at school where they live (which is mainly in the Andean Highlands).

Efforts to connect, inform and also entertain existing and potential users often go alongside activities to secure the legal status of a language and, hence, its endorsement in a country or region. An example is Scottish Gaelic, whose BBC Alba television has news, sport, music and entertainment programmes in the language. With a following of about 80,000 speakers, the channel has a small audience, but its Twitter feed attracts 2,000 followers in the language (that is, one in forty speakers). This virtual forum can bring together the language communities from both Scotland and Canada (mainly Nova Scotia). Scottish Gaelic enjoys minority status on both sides of the Atlantic. In Europe, it is promoted as one of around sixty indigenous languages that are included under the European Charter for Regional or Minority Languages.[30] The World Language Advancement Act[31] that has been proposed in the United States might, with the will of speakers, also work in favour of several Alaskan Native and American Indian languages. But to be effective, such measures need an economic dimension and the inclusion of the relevant languages in key institutional domains, including public administration and the media.

Of course, it would be impossible to cater equally for every language. It is partly in response to global threats to biodiversity that cultural and linguistic ecosystems have come to be regarded as part of fragile environments that are worth preserving. The concept of language diversity is also embedded in wider notions of diversity that originated in collective demands made by social movements related to anti-racism and multiculturalism in the 1970s and 1980s. The dominant discourse on diversity has since then revolved around notions premised on reducing inequality and discrimination and developing 'inclusivity' (e.g. in and through schooling). But the practical application of language diversity principles can falter on the basis of cost.

Clearly, language diversity is nothing new. But the mix now experienced in many industrialized societies has increased drastically through globalization and mass travel.

Furthermore, in the European Union, the members' cross-border rights of passage add to this 'linguistic salad bowl'.[32] 'Superdiversity' is another term that has been coined to capture the mobile, diffuse cultural mix that characterizes our urban environments.[33] For example, today, a third of Londoners (around 2.5 million people) are foreign born, encompassing more than 270 nationalities and 300 languages.[34] Hosting people from all over the world entails providing them with schools, healthcare, housing and access to information. But the operational logistics of providing such diverse public services are often difficult, with authorities also facing budgetary constraints.

This wide range of scenarios points to the complex nature and partnership of languages and economics. There are those who believe that investment in inclusive policies to support language diversity could benefit society in the long run. But what practices are there to optimize the market potential of language diversity, and how can these enhance economic and personal growth? In the context of globalization, language resources are more mobile than ever before. Hence, patterns of language use have become less predictable. The challenge, then, to be explored now, is to find ways of capturing existing language resources of mobile speakers in mobile markets.

CHAPTER THREE

Managing multilingualism

'What does "pull up" mean?' These are the last recorded words of a Chinese pilot as he attempted to land a US-made McDonnell Douglas MD-80 jet airliner.[1] Unable to understand the audio alarm, he crashed in Ürümqi, northwestern China, on 13 November 1993, with fatal consequences for twelve of the 102 passengers and crew. This tragic incident of miscommunication is sadly not unique in aviation history.

Errors in communication or lack of understanding caused by language barriers have led to many types of failures, including lost business deals, mistakes in medical procedures and the compromise of security. The potential for accidents and misunderstandings is highest in multilingual contexts. The cost, a kind of covert 'language tax', is the other side of the coin of multilingualism.

Dealing with communication problems in multilanguage settings is a practical challenge. Investment in language training would seem to be a rational move to mitigate the risks of multiple languages used in the public domain, in areas as diverse as safety, sales and security. But are organizations up to it? Some enterprises may be reluctant to release funds for such support unless the gains are quantifiable and, preferably, immediate.[2] Other companies have a clear language strategy and invest large sums in upgrading their employees' language skills. The application of measures for effective communication in a multilingual environment is an example of language management. Had the Chinese pilot been given the necessary language support, fatalities would almost certainly have been avoided. The monetary and social implications of language diversity policies and practices can be far reaching.

Lessons from failures

As we travel, we are likely to come across a diverse mosaic of languages. In many cases, our communication will be seamless, so we may not even be aware of language choices made. So booking a holiday in an Austrian ski resort will be done via a carefully crafted website that has four or five language buttons to ensure a smooth visit. Similarly, calling that Indonesian hotel to ask them if they have found your wallet that you think you left in the bar is likely to be made easier if the desk clerk is able to fluidly switch to English. However, things may not work out so well in situations when you are away from the tourist trail. You may encounter a language problem when you need to report to the police in a suburb of Tokyo about a robbery you experienced there, or explain your next of kin's medical history to health professionals in one of Kiev's hospitals for an emergency operation.

Clearly, language issues in the modern world are not just about tourism. What would you do if you are about to strike an export deal for your company but you have become suspicious about your Brazilian trade partners' recent business dealings during dinner the night before? Having to deal with such a challenge at short notice is another example of language management. It might have been a good idea to pay for an interpreter to avoid this problem in the first place. Perhaps you have a backup plan. You may be able to exchange information with a degree of, possibly reciprocal, accommodation towards the language of your potential business partners. So you stick to your own language (French) and they use theirs (Portuguese). Both of you may have to speak more slowly and clearly or use simple structures. Alternatively, you might apply the same technique with your limited Portuguese, or they might do so using French. Or else, the mutual exchange may be in a mixture of both languages. If this type of approach is not feasible, resorting to another language you both share (say, German) may be an option.

These are some of the means we can spontaneously adopt when faced with an emergency in a multilingual setting. Where time and circumstances permit, portable electronic means may be able to provide further, almost instantaneous, assistance. But languages are processed in particular ways in such cases and vital details may, as they say, get lost in translation, resulting in misunderstandings. Problems with multilingual communication can have a range of adverse social and economic effects, hindering trade, lowering productivity and compromising safety. In each case, different language management strategies may be invoked in order to minimize the risks of failures and accidents.

Gaps, needs, practices

Communication difficulties in multilingual contexts are linked to a wide range of transportation accidents around the world, as was the case in Ürümqi. Direct evidence of disastrous effects through miscommunication comes from 'black box' recordings in the aviation industry. Accident investigations have linked ineffective exchanges between pilots and air traffic controllers with fateful decisions and air crashes such as the 1977 aircraft collision at Tenerife airport in the Canary Islands, in which 583 passengers died. Two Boeing 747 jumbo jets had been diverted to Tenerife by a bomb blast at their intended destination of Gran Canaria International airport. Poor weather conditions, ineffective communication and imprecise terminology used in exchanges between the Dutch

KLM crew, an American Pan Am crew and a Spanish air traffic controller led to the worst ever disaster in aviation history.[3]

The risks caused by miscommunication in air travel have been calculated using incident records in NASA's Aviation Safety Reporting System, the world's largest repository of airline safety information. The analysis puts incorrect or incomplete pilot/controller communications as a causal or circumstantial factor in 70–80 per cent of incidents or accidents. Sufficient proficiency in English, the de facto language of intercommunication in the airline industry, is essential for reasons of passenger safety. In some instances, problems with communication in the cockpit are further exacerbated through cultural and hierarchical differences between the pilot and co-pilot. Such cultural clashes were identified to have played a role in a series of air crashes that plagued Korean Air in the 1980s.[4]

Since that time, various systems have been put in place to enhance safety in the aviation domain. Flight operators worldwide now lay greater emphasis on language requirements (use of both English as a common working language and standard phrases) for effective pilot/controller communications. To overcome possible language barriers, American crews in an Airbus flying over other countries must now also develop an ability to understand a non-native controller's accented English instructions. Furthermore, to ensure that end users (pilots and airline crews) easily recognize data, Airbus has produced voice-to-text software that provides pilots with regular information such as wind speeds, temperatures and altitude levels during flights.[5] Aviation-specific information and accent recognition technologies that capture voice messages between ground staff and the crew and display them as text are also being incorporated to enhance safety.

In their production processes, too, multinational companies are dependent on a common language for labelling parts. This requires considerable coordination in major enterprises with manufacturing bases in different countries. Airbus assembles in France airplane components that are shipped in from different countries – Germany, Spain, Wales and England. Engineers in the plants in Nantes and Toulouse need to be able to understand the various instructions from Hamburg, Madrid, Broughton (in North Wales) and Filton (near Bristol, UK) on how all the different aircraft parts are meant to be fitted together. Clear and unambiguous translations that use systematic terminology are essential in this line of work.

In maritime transportation, too, though they are less well-documented, ineffective verbal exchanges between multinational crews are known to compromise safety. Shipping companies expect that individual crew members should be able to carry out orders in a common working language (which is often that of the country where the ship is registered) for effective day-to-day on-board operations. But the potential for communication difficulties at sea is high in cases where, as often happens, there may be on board no more than a handful of individuals from any one country. The results of miscommunication at sea that have been reported range from mild annoyance to the creation of potentially hazardous situations.[6] The use of standard maritime vocabulary is also promoted to ensure successful logistical emergency operations under stressful circumstances – for example, when manoeuvrability has become restricted, or when a fuel tank spill has been detected or when a salvage operation caused by a collision is being carried out. The potential for maritime accidents has been found to increase in communications from ship to ship in areas of congestion or from ship to shore in port operations and for rescue activities where little time or space can be afforded for mistakes to be made.[7] Clearly, in emergencies, the potential for human error is raised and, hence, communication needs to be well managed. This is especially the case where the demands of talking in another language can stretch individuals' ability to express themselves coherently and competently.

Similarly, a crew member's lack of ability to understand written safety instructions can have fatal consequences, as happened on board the MV Unitas in Mostyn port on 10 July 1994:

> The German vessel Unitas was manned with German officers and Kiribati crew. The crew had not received work safety instructions in English and had insufficient information in English concerning the dangerous cargo. It was due to this that a crewmember entered a hatch although it was dangerous and forbidden. He was asphyxiated in the hatch and lost his life along with the chief officer who had gone in to try to save him.[8]

Between vessels at sea, a well-established backup means of conveying essential communication is through flags using the International Code of Signals. This is employed to transmit important maritime messages, using a combination of up to seven flags. The origins of this 'silent language of ships' go back to the sixteenth century when more frequent sailings of bigger vessels required ship-to-ship contact at sea. The international flag system used nowadays focuses on navigation and safety, including medical emergencies, or occasions when military ships wish to maintain radio silence. For example, the red flag (signifying the letter 'b') when hoisted alerts approaching ships with the (encoded) message: 'I am carrying, loading or discharging dangerous goods.' Similarly, in aviation, a system of red, white and green flashing lights is used when other means of communication fail between aircraft and the ground.

Communication problems are especially acute at the healthcare frontline where, increasingly, travellers from all parts of the world present themselves, often in 'extremis'. This can be a major problem since, normally, 80 per cent of a diagnosis is based on a patient's history (the remaining 20 per cent comes from an examination). When medical practitioners share no language with their patients, they may use gestures (in the words of one clinician, 'go veterinary'[9]) or try and find someone who can interpret. But there are risks in terms of privacy if a family member is approached for this purpose and in terms of accuracy in the interpretation of medical terminology.

Usually, when communication during a medical consultation is limited, there will be a greater reliance on tests. But this can slow diagnosis and treatment. Ideally, in healthcare, patients should be offered an equitable service as defined by need, including mediation by a professional interpreter if required. However, the level of this type of provision varies greatly between countries. The UK's National Health Service (NHS) sets an example in its commitment to this core principle, but the extent of services covered is continually under pressure. With developments in mobile health (mHealth), there are new possibilities in the supply of patient-centred care in multilingual contexts. One means to offer language support in the care supply chain is through telemedicine, which has been adopted as an integrated strategy in Italy after a trial phase in the city of Bologna.[10] This works through a flexible computer-based multi-user system where health concerns can be discussed in a range of languages.

Among other practices to limit adverse health outcomes through miscommunication is usage of an internal translation service during working hours. An alternative means is a dedicated three-way telephone interpreting service (for instance *LanguageLine)*, which operates with dual handsets that allow clinicians and patients to interact with each other via a distant interpreter.[11] The problem with this system is that it uses up precious time, which is almost always in short supply in healthcare settings. Chiefly, language support services need to be available round the clock to make a difference to clinical care and health outcomes, particularly in emergencies. Where this is not possible, Google Translate may plug the gaps in a range of languages. I spoke to a clinician on a busy hospital ward who talked about a situation she encountered, which illustrates this point:

> I was in A&E looking after a patient who had water on her lungs. She needed a tube to be inserted into her chest in

order to drain off the fluid and alleviate her symptoms and I needed her consent for this procedure. It was 3.00 a.m. and her family had gone home. The patient was illiterate, didn't speak a word of English, and there was nobody around who could translate into Gujarati. The situation was really frustrating because her symptoms were troubling her and I wanted to help. I tried a few translation websites but it was taking too long. My senior told me that we had more urgent things to attend to, as she was stable and could wait until the morning. A few hours later, on the consultant ward round, my senior and I felt really embarrassed when our consultant simply whipped out his smartphone and used Google Translate to speak to her verbally. He gained consent within minutes.[12]

Multiple language needs are especially marked in the case of patients who are refugees or asylum seekers, some of whom have complex, serious and frequently stigmatizing conditions such as TB, HIV or mental health problems. Treating vulnerable groups of people with complex medical and social needs will often put further pressure on an already stretched healthcare system.

Away from healthcare, miscommunication is also known to be an issue in industry. Whether in construction, the oil and gas sectors or in high-risk chemical plants, an ever-changing multilingual workforce can be found. In many such workplaces, foreign contractors, technical staff and manual workers hired on a short-term basis are exposed to hazardous substances. But some may not be able to understand the language of the handling instructions. These employees depend on clear documentation of their on-site operating tasks, particularly when it comes to the labelling and packaging of chemical mixtures.

In such multilingual workplaces, language barriers can occur in speech, signage and gestures (or their written equivalents). The resulting miscommunication risks include inefficiency, unsafe situations and accidents. If these language issues are also coupled with illiteracy in some of the workforce, then dealing with differential oral and written abilities of employees requires more immediate action to prevent failures and losses. Analysis of safety documents written for process plants in the Netherlands has shown that these can be difficult for the workforce and visitors to understand.[13] Companies have responded to these risks in a number of ways, for example, by producing additional safety documentation with graphic displays.

The Dutch findings also suggest that industrial accident investigation methods frequently underestimate the effect of language issues in multilanguage worksites. This has relevance for policymaking since businesses are bound by law to keep their employees safe from harm. In particular, to guide language-related safety procedures in plants, regulations have been issued as part of the newly revised 2015 EU Seveso III Directive on the prevention and control of industrial accidents in companies.[14]

Of course, it could be argued that process plants, building sites, and oil and gas sites are inherently dangerous places, and that accidents are inevitable. After all, such workplaces can exhibit a plethora of time-critical problems and safety hazards. This includes the risk of falling objects, unguarded machinery, working at heights or underground services where workers are exposed in confined spaces to the possibility of floods, electrocution or even explosion. Such industries have a patchy safety record worldwide. For example, there has recently been a high incidence of casualties and fatalities in Qatar involving foreign (mainly Indian and Nepalese) workers hired on low pay and without exit visas, for building the football stadia for the 2022 World Cup.[15] Much of the terrible safety record in Qatar appears to be related to undue pressure, cutting corners and a general lack of concern for worker welfare. How do we know that such accidents were language related?

Recent fieldwork carried out in the UK has shown that the risk of on-site accidents and fatalities is especially high for foreign construction workers with low English language ability. The twelve migrant worker deaths that figured in a report on incidents in 2007 and 2008 represented 17 per cent of the total number of fatalities, which is, at the very least, twice what should be expected when compared with control groups. Of these accidents, most happened during the victims' first week at work. On-site induction is usually offered for migrants, but this has been observed to vary in terms of delivery and format, often aiming to 'get all [the migrants] through' quickly.[16]

Many major contractors are starting to pay greater attention to challenges with communication on their multilanguage worksites to reduce health and safety risks and, also, to secure the uninterrupted flow of production processes. Some of them are investing in a range of means to improve in-house occupational communication among employees, notably through translation, training and signage. Other initiatives include having foremen who are able to interpret interactions on the shop floor between colleagues from different language backgrounds. More informally, many workplaces run buddy schemes with employees acting as language and cultural brokers among colleagues.

An example of good practice in the attempt to lower occupational risks through miscommunication is the Dutch 'language barrier' project.[17] With trade union funding, this scheme offers a toolkit that has been created with input from a consortium of companies in the metalworking and technological industries to improve workplace safety and efficiency. The first of the recommended measures is to determine the organization's working language (which may or may not be that of the company's location). The aim is to streamline task-oriented communication between employees. In practice, workers are also provided with a handheld device that has a translation tool and an (expandable) online dictionary with multilingual documentation including pictograms to show what tasks need to be done and how. These short-term support systems are followed up in due course with language training that matches the work skills for bidirectional communication and feedback. With organizational backing, prototypes such as this could also be adapted for use in other multilingual workplace settings across the world, especially where financial and staffing problems lead to large-scale recruitment of temporary personnel from different language backgrounds. Although such schemes cost money both to set up and to run, they make economic sense since workers who can communicate with each other will work better together than when they are not able to do so.

Challenges and opportunities

The range of language diversity–related challenges outlined so far barely scratches the surface of existing communication gaps and needs. As a result, the overall societal and economic impact is only beginning to be grasped. Moreover, in health and social care provision, and in many other parts of the public sector, the pressures on services are often hidden and, hence, not easily identifiable. Frequently, there will be a focus on 'getting on with the job' until, within available budgets, a critical point is reached when action plans are needed for good practice to be maintained.

Not much is known about the return on investment of different language support systems used in multilingual environments for service provision, administration and infrastructure. This is largely because, as noted before, such an assessment would be difficult to carry out since any costs and benefits involve not only financial but also social aspects that cannot easily be calculated. A pragmatic, time-honoured approach is for workplaces to improve on-site communication by tapping into existing language resources and using the skills of bilingual staff. As well as being immediate, this option is usually cost-effective, since the bilingual workers may do this task as part of their job. Organizations that realize their employees' full potential in this way may, in turn, transform the way in which they work.

Naturally, language needs are more complex in urban environments with their ever-changing social ecologies. In many ways, cities with a multilingual profile are in a better position to attract foreign investment, especially in favourable tax regimes. But, as is widely acknowledged, the benefits that come from hosting able people from different cultural backgrounds also entail obligations as regards the well-being of the incoming population. In particular, a significant level of commitment to language support is needed in order to ensure equal access to public services. Some cosmopolitan hubs such as San Francisco, Melbourne and New York have explicitly formulated policies for a wholesale allocation of resources to facilitate interpreting and translation, together with other additional outreach support[18] for the deaf or hard of hearing. By contrast, London is one of many cities that have a decentralized approach to decisions about language provision for its heterogeneous population. In the absence of a coordinated strategy, support mechanisms are more locally defined and can vary considerably. For example, in dense multilanguage environments such as London's Tower Hamlets, many residents will require an interpreter's assistance to deal with matters such as social benefits, healthcare and job seekers' allowance.

Increasingly, organizations and institutions are displaying resourcefulness in finding ways of supplying their services to customers speaking diverse languages. In the public sector, the police, fire and rescue services and medical surgeries rely on multilingual staff and sometimes on volunteers from community centres for communication. However, to ensure impartiality with suspects or confidentiality with patients in the police or medical services, respectively, interpreters are often hired on a commercial basis. Another means of ensuring equal access to public services is providing people with multilingual leaflets or brochures that are made available widely free of charge. This is common practice in the social, healthcare and legal services where advice is dispensed in this way in a range of languages, on diverse issues such as diabetes, hypertension, asthma, abuse, divorce, housing or depression. In addition, multilingual notices are often used in public spaces with significant levels of footfall, such as airports, hospitals, tourist areas or commercial zones. The languages employed on such signage normally reflect the concentration of people found to be using these premises. An example can be found at the top of the Swiss mountain Titlis. Its panoramic setting has been chosen for many years as a safe location to film scenes for Bollywood movies, at a time when the natural setting of the disputed area of Kashmir is deemed to be too dangerous for the actors and crew. Such is the draw of these films that fans are happy to travel thousands of miles from Asia to Switzerland to the top of the Titlis, where they are greeted with signage in Hindi,[19] Chinese and Korean as well as the expected equivalents in English, French, German and Portuguese. Such multilingual support practices that confront diversity challenges in public spaces also give a boost to tourist resorts and cities, helping them prosper in the international arena, both socially and economically.

In many urban environments, numerous grassroots initiatives have been launched using existing language resources to support language needs across a wide range of contexts on an ad hoc basis. An example is 'Migrants for Migrants' (Mi-Mi), a proactive scheme for foreign workers in Germany.[20] This mobilizes, trains and certifies bilingual migrants to act as cultural brokers and go-betweens for members of their own communities and various service providers of their host country. A responsive project, this also assists foreign healthcare users in dealing with day-to-day health issues and handling emergencies. Other means of support are through social media and online exchange sites such as the user-led 'Welcoming Migrants and Refugees Forum' that links newcomers with organizations.[21]

Similar localized practices exist in the education sphere. For example, in some of the UK's major cities such as Birmingham and Manchester, different immigrant communities (who make up about a third of the total urban population) are operating supplementary classes in their own languages (notably in Punjabi, Bengali, Somali, Hindi, Gujarati, Arabic and Chinese) to complement mainstream education.[22] Such schemes that draw on the native skills of individuals have proved to be an effective way of putting local resources into practice. Notably, this can help reduce social inequalities by targeting language disparities.

With multilingualism becoming a daily reality for many, cities are natural hotspots for creative ideas in support of language diversity. Many such activities are eminently transferable from one setting to another. Under the motto 'Cities as Drivers for Quality Jobs and Sustainable Growth', the European Union's EUROCITIES network aims to enhance visibility of good practice in this area.[23] A forum for creative citizenship, it coordinates exchange of responsive urban initiatives in the realms of employment, schools, housing and well-being, and also in dealing with health inequalities and illiteracies. As one of its objectives, it supports flexible language management schemes to facilitate communication between people from different cultural backgrounds. A range of major cities across Europe, from Reykjavik in Iceland, to Odessa in the Ukraine and Sarajevo in Bosnia and Herzegovina have joined in the exchange and transfer of knowledge to help the planning of their own localized practices.

One of this network's current projects, 'Culture for Cities and Regions', seeks to identify successful examples of schemes that promote investment in creative industries for local economic development and urban regeneration.[24] This suggests that grassroots initiatives that use multilingualism innovatively as a tool may well work to strengthen transurban economic and cultural relations. However, informal urban language management measures such as these are subject to the temporary nature of available human resources and, hence, they need to be flexible. Nevertheless, such local practices that bring together ideas and use talents from across different language communities may well provide a model for inspired overall policymaking.

Bridging across languages

The story of the Tower of Babel is usually understood as a biblical explanation for the diversity of languages.

> Now the whole world had one language and a common speech. They said to each other: 'Come, let's make bricks and bake them thoroughly.' … Then they said: 'Come, let us build ourselves a city, with a tower that reaches to the heavens, so that we may make a name for ourselves.' … The Lord said: '*If as one people speaking the same language they have begun to do this, then nothing they plan to do will be impossible for them. Come, let us go down and confuse their language so they will not understand each other*' [my italics]. So the Lord scattered them … and they left off to build the city.[25]

Among the many interpretations of the 'Babylonian confusion' is the one that because people were no longer able to understand each other, they could not co-operate or be productive. The communication barriers led to the breakup of an ambitious building project[26] (the Tower of Babel was never finished). Illustrating the 'potential for damage of a multilingual work setting',[27] this narrative readily applies to real challenges today, as seen on construction sites.

We learn from the story that God was worried about the power that a single language gave to men. As Steven Pinker put it: 'A common language connects the members of a community into an information-sharing network with formidable collective powers.'[28] Clearly, a common language is an efficient system of communication and, hence, has utility value. It is needed for safety in international travel as we saw in the case of aviation or shipping. Also, in cross-border commerce, it adds no extra costs to transactions and enhances competition. Would society at large, in the context of globalization, fare better with fewer languages, or maybe even with just one language? But which language would best serve as a lingua franca? Would you be happy to give up English (the language of this book) and learn another language that was deemed to be universally more useful? And what of the scale of the task of adopting *one* language worldwide?

In fact, an attempt was made over one hundred years ago to *create* a new language that could be used by everyone. In the late nineteenth century, Esperanto was intended to foster human understanding through a culturally neutral language that unites rather than divides. But it has not become a universal second language as its founder Zamenhof had hoped when he proposed it as a 'Lingvo Internacia'.[29] It might have had a chance, however. In 1921, the Chairman of the Paris Chamber of Commerce recommended that its members should use Esperanto as an auxiliary language. The plan was to institute Esperanto classes in all the Chamber's business schools so that students could learn and use it for commercial purposes. M. André Baudet, Chairman of the Steering Committee, who described Esperanto as an international code rather than a language, said: 'It won't revolutionise the world, and there is no likelihood that it will take the place of any language, but ... it can be useful to every people and aid enormously in international business [enabling it to be carried out] without error, faster and cheaper.'[30] But in the following year, at a sitting on the question of international languages, the League of Nations rejected the idea of introducing Esperanto as an international business language. Nevertheless, Esperanto has by now been established in some quarters. It is a means of instruction at the Academy of Sciences in San Marino and it is also offered as a foreign language in Hungarian schools. Moreover, it has a presence on Google Translate.

In today's international market the more likely choice for a single universal language would be English with its estimated 840 million users. However, in many parts of the world, knowledge of English is less widespread than is sometimes assumed. According to the CIA World Fact Book, well over two-thirds of the world's population do not speak English.[31]

This includes chiefly the older age groups, those in blue-collar jobs and some nationalities (e.g. speakers of Romance languages, Spanish, Italian and French).

How about Mandarin, China's official language? With well over one billion users, it features highly in managers' preferences for doing business with the world's most populous and economically dynamic nation. But, as already discussed in Chapter 1, connecting trade forecasts with particular language training needs requires a far-sighted perspective, given the unpredictability of economic developments. Will China remain competitive, or is it in a phase of unsustainable growth that will be followed by the inevitable collapse and loss of productivity, just as ambitious businessmen are finishing off their Business Mandarin modules on their smartphones?

Future changes in the global economy may shift the balance from the EU and ASEAN trade blocks to expanding markets in other parts of the world (perhaps the CIVETS or EAGLEs groups mentioned in Chapter 2). This might mean that in the longer term, the current language use dynamics could change in accordance with the way upcoming growth centres choose to position themselves on the world stage of economics. With this in mind, investing in a number of different languages would seem pertinent as many businesses have owners, investors and overseas customers speaking different languages. It is reasonable to assume, then, that multilingualism is here to stay and that the adoption of one universal language is not going to serve a society's economy, at least for the foreseeable future. So what is the best strategy to cover such diversity, in essence to cope with the legacy of the Tower of Babel, in the era of mass communication and globalization?

As we have already seen, the promotion of multilingualism as a policy option is formally practised in a number of countries worldwide. Various models exist to suit local contexts. Switzerland paved the way by enshrining official multilingualism in its 1848 constitution. Other countries have since followed, for example, Singapore with four languages (English, Malay, Tamil, Standard Mandarin) and South Africa with eleven (including

English, Afrikaans, Zulu, Sotho and Ndebele). These nationally selected languages usually feature as the media of public communication and in education, law and administration. Where English forms part of the official language package, it tends to be the choice for business and economic relations. However, such policy choices might well change because these models, cast pre-globalization, may not be considered sustainable in the future. This sentiment is reflected in the recent rejection of French as the second language taught in schools by the voters in Switzerland's German-speaking canton Zurich, and its replacement by English (not yet an official Swiss language).

In practice, national language policies have produced two striking paradoxes: On the one hand, in territorially multilingual countries such as Belgium or Switzerland, some individuals can go through life as monoglots, relatively untouched by the cosmopolitan language practices in Antwerp or Bruxelles, Zurich or Geneva. On the other hand, in officially monolingual states with traditional and migrant language communities, for example in Germany, France or Greece, multilingualism can be widespread.

Conversely, in countries with composite cultures and a high degree of historically rooted language diversity, and in many postcolonial settings, individual bilingualism and multilingualism is a social need. A case in point is India with an estimated 1,365 indigenous languages, where many individuals will have some mastery of both their local and state languages (which may not be the same) and also of Hindi and English for wider communication. Similarly, in Tanzania, a country with speakers of 126 major indigenous languages, people will use English and Swahili nationally and for communication with other populations, plus various regional and local languages on the home front. These are places where the culturally embedded, traditional languages have a mainly regional currency.

Other culturally mixed countries have an *apparent* monolingualism. For example, the United States is a land teeming with many different languages, but English is predominant. Australia has a similar history. But there is a linguistic Pandora's Box lying buried under the veneer of this apparent language uniformity. English unifies but at the same time homogenizes the different indigenous and immigrant cultures. Yet, as we have seen, tapping into such diversity can have economic benefits. So how can this diversity be exploited while still retaining national unity? This question may well have to be faced soon, as both US and Australian demographics evolve. With their imported language diversity, in both Australia and the United States, there is a sense of a tipping point, where innovative ideas are waiting to be tapped into once the monolingual mask slips. In Australia, there have been moves to utilize the vast skills pool for outward communication. A wider appreciation that languages are a vital national resource could be of relevance in the United States, too. But to become a social resource, this requires sustained support, without which it can be a negative feature that leads to ghettoization and exclusion. If properly managed through education and in the workplace, this may well serve economic interests, as well as strategic and security needs. But as large federalist countries, Australia and the United States have dispersed jurisdictions that preserve relatively autonomous authority, and, hence, language planning is more loosely coordinated than if it were managed centrally as, say, in France.

The economic dimension of languages can give a strong impetus for politicians to launch dual language initiatives and get them democratically accepted. This is happening in Saarland, a region of Germany that borders France. Recently, President Annegret Kramp-Karrenbauer introduced a policy that would lead to full bilingualism with French within three decades (by 2043).[32] The plan is to achieve this through schooling and, in the first instance, through a cross-border exchange of personnel as an immediate prerequisite to foster trade with neighbouring Lorraine in France. She sees this 'France-competence' as a unique selling point for her region, making Saarland indispensable and inevitable as a bridge to Germany from France and a gateway to France from Germany. This example shows how a local economic rationale can make bilingualism a desirable goal for adjoining monolingual nations or regions. To take effect, this policy will need to be maintained and spread via appropriate measures in political and social institutions as well as the public media. Naturally, schools and higher educational institutions function as the core agencies in the development of such multilingual capabilities.

Investing in human capital

All of us coming together on this page have benefitted from some form of human capital investment: you, reading this book, perhaps in a language other than your own; me, drawing on my expertise as a linguist to write it; the publishers, using their desktop creativity for its production. We have acquired our skills through education, training and, above all, experience. This has equipped us with the resources we require to be productive, to read, to write and to interact with others. We have had to invest time and money in learning these skills. We may already have recovered this outlay, or may be able to do so later. Economists define expenditures on education and training as investments in human capital.[33] Few people would challenge the appropriateness, in principle, of studying other languages to supplement their existing means of communication. Rather, the issues are the following: How should additional language education be facilitated, from what age and at what cost?

Languages in schools

School children in many countries around the world learn a second language at an early age. Across the EU member states, more than 80 per cent are already doing so in elementary school. In parts of Spain, this starts from the age of three, in Denmark at kindergarten, and in Italy, Luxembourg, Malta and Norway at age six. This second language is mostly English (95 per cent), followed mainly by French (24 per cent), German (16 per cent) and Spanish (11 per cent). In many cases, a second language is added by the age of ten and a third one before pupils reach the age of fifteen.[34] Elsewhere too, in Australia, Hong Kong, New Zealand and Singapore, the trend is to learn additional languages at a young age. Early exposure to different languages in many ways exploits young children's natural curiosity, which may, in turn, aid their cognitive development. Moreover, it will give them a stronger foundation to build on at the secondary level as adaptable individuals.

There is also a move in many countries to offer a greater number of languages, with attention often given to market forces. It was mainly an economic incentive that propelled the introduction of Asian languages in Australia's schools. A language skills deficit in the United States has also generated calls for more language education at schools, including Arabic, in addition to Spanish.[35] In the West, as we have seen, Mandarin is gaining ground among the range of additional languages featured at school. Conversely, in East Asia, English is becoming more widespread at the primary level, with children learning it in China, South Korea, Japan, Taiwan and elsewhere. This move in schools towards teaching economically more salient languages can be a point of contention. In quadrilingual Switzerland, for example, the replacement of a second national language in the curriculum with English has been met in some quarters with fears over possible adverse effects on social cohesion within the country. The fundamental approach to the choice of language curricula in schools seems to be that of suiting regional conditions, but within a global context. At its most basic level, this could mean offering pupils the chance to learn a language of a neighbouring country and also a global language (in addition to their own), as is promoted in the European Union.[36]

A big question for those planning investment in languages for schools is whether multiple language skills are less relevant in countries where English is used officially. Because of its de facto status as a common language internationally, there is often little interest in studying other languages in Anglophone countries. A case in point is the United States, where no nationwide second-language mandate exists at any level of education. Initiatives there to introduce the study of different languages at school have often lacked support and are affected by budget cuts. A proactive push in support of language learning programmes in elementary and secondary schools has been made with a proposed World Language Advancement Act.[37] To increase its chance of becoming an Act of Congress, its advocates suggest that expanding opportunities to learn different languages will prepare and equip the future generation of American workers with linchpin skills needed to compete in the knowledge economy.

This pragmatic focus has encountered challenges of a different type in parts of the United States. Students in Oklahoma's high schools are now allowed to use computer programming course credits to fulfil their state's foreign language graduation requirement.[38] This idea has also caught on in a number of other states including Florida, Kentucky, New Mexico and Texas, with proponents arguing that learning computer 'languages' such as C/C++, Java or Python prepares pupils better for the twenty-first century workplace where such skills are regularly used. Programming 'languages' clearly have utility value, and 'multi-coding' capabilities also reflect positively on employability. However, many would argue that a computer code is not a language.[39] Certainly, it is a written set of instructions with its own internal logic, so it would appear to have some aspects of human language. But a programming 'language' is only a one-way method of communication and lacks the subtleties of human interaction.

Conversely, in Australia, the learning of languages other than English (LOTE) in schools has enjoyed long-term support.[40] This has in the past focused on the languages of various major communities, such as Greek in Melbourne, Italian in Sydney and German in Adelaide. The government has invested significant sums (around A$60 million) in its recent move to include Mandarin, Indonesian, Japanese and Korean in the curriculum as priority languages. Nevertheless, in the last decade, the take-up rate of these languages has decreased in schools despite the rise of the targeted Asian economies as a possible incentive.[41] This development is partly due to the fact that these languages are culturally more distant and are perceived as difficult to learn.

Language decisions in education also revolve around the language(s) used as the means of instruction. This can be a global, neighbouring or a minority language. Different models of schooling are used for children from minority language backgrounds, depending on student numbers, available resources (teachers and learning materials) and budgets. In some places, for example in many post-Soviet settings, language-rich education systems serve to cater for diverse communities who have coexisted there for a long time. Lithuania's education programme covers four minority languages, Romania's includes eleven and the Ukraine's supports fourteen.[42] Various bilingual models exist as regards the length and intensity of teaching offered in the mother tongue, alongside education in the majority language. The longer a dual (mother tongue plus majority language) teaching system continues, the greater the chance that students will end up with full proficiency and literacy in two languages. Conversely, programmes that allow early exit from the mother tongue tend to lead to linguistic assimilation into the majority language in due course. Apart from the recognized cognitive benefits that arise for learners through bilingual education,[43] these models can serve as a means to open up social and career benefits and unlock economic marginalization.

Across the world, in countries with traditionally composite cultures such as India, Mexico or Brazil, parents often prefer their children to be taught in the medium of an economically dominant language rather than in their mother tongue.

Opportunism and economic incentives dictate that proficiency in, say, Lomwe in Mozambique or Mapudungun in Chile brings the next generation fewer advantages than competence in Portuguese or Spanish, or even English. A case in point is the drive in Indian schools away from lesser-used native languages towards English as well as Hindi, Bengali, Tamil and Urdu. Such language choices in education frequently result in response to market-driven values. Among the anticipated tangible benefits for learners are upward social mobility, greater employment prospects and access to wider markets. These expected social returns partly explain the high value that the ex-colonial languages have retained.

These educational scenarios show how language education choices are often governed by a pragmatic focus on the 'utility' and economic potential of languages. Similarly, with growing competition and emerging markets, economic factors are gaining importance in debates on language curricula and are shaping national education policy. But, as has already been shown in Australia, economically motivated initiatives that promote learning of culturally distant languages may not succeed in attracting sufficient interest, despite the market incentive. By only looking at a country's GDP as an indicator for a language's 'worth', we may omit from the calculation the sociocultural aspect of languages. Schemes that form part of ongoing local economic developments such as that in German Saarland look promising, since the cultural distance between neighbours is not so great.

At any rate, the widely felt push for multilingual schooling reflects the recognition that multilanguage capabilities are needed in the modern world. Gaining ground in education, too, is the idea that an individual's (partial) skills in different languages can constitute a 'composite' resource.[44] According to this, persons with varying proficiency levels in, say, French, English and Italian can in certain contexts creatively activate their abilities as a single, functional competence. For example, you would be likely to make yourself understood in the train station of Florence if you were to ask: 'Quelle heure ultimo train?' This approach to language use mirrors that of the original lingua franca and is thought to have productive potential. It represents a shift away from a view of multilingual skills as distinct abilities to one that focuses on the actual, accumulated multiple repertoires of speakers.

Tertiary education

In response to globalization, many governments around the world, from Malaysia to Canada to The Gambia, are making an effort to internationalize tertiary education. This expanding sector is seen as a market opportunity, bolstered by more and more institutions keen to attract foreign students with a widening range of accredited courses at about twice the cost (currently about US $19,000 in the United States) of home fees. The incomers' interest mainly comes in response to a university's reputation and international profile as outwardly manifested on elaborate websites, usually with a version in English. These outside investors also put money into the local economy in the form of day-to-day living expenses. In addition, these future alumni may in due course respond to the experience they obtained in their alma mater by becoming generous benefactors.

This globalization of tertiary education has led to a number of different ways in which course programmes are being reorganized to meet the newly emerging needs of international students. In particular, the academic community is reshaping the means by which languages are offered for both specialist study and basic key skills. Packaged as joint degree courses of the 'French with Business' type, languages are now marketed more as a commodity. In technical subjects, too, languages are routinely offered as an add-on to a degree to help bolster career prospects, whether for engineers, doctors or scientists. Such institution-wide language provision has grown rapidly in recent years in response to student demand while the numbers enrolling on specialist language degrees have declined. This shift shows that students view languages less as a vocation and more as a tool.

Attempting to boost their shrinking market share, traditional language departments are now also emphasizing utility: 'This degree is extremely wide ranging in its scope and opens up countless career opportunities'[45] (Modern and Medieval Languages, Cambridge); 'Over 80 per cent of our alumni today are employed or professionally active in their chosen disciplines'[46] (Near Eastern Languages and Civilizations, Yale). Clearly, the role of languages in enhancing employability skills and competencies of students is a firmly embedded marketing tag in the higher education sector.

The language revolution in the tertiary market has even reached areas that might appear to be resistant to such change. Some universities are setting up campuses in overseas countries to provide a conduit from new markets to their home base. Others are teaching some courses in English to attract more students. In Japan, the 'Global 30' project has recently been launched with the slogan: 'No Japanese proficiency required at the time of admission.'[47] The country's top universities are now offering entire degree programmes in English, breaking down the language barrier that was once an obstacle preventing international students from studying in Japan. Similarly, the new Skolkovo Institute of Science and Technology (Skoltech), a private graduate research university near Moscow, is branching out to provide 'a hands-on experience in brand-new facilities with world-class professors – all in English'.[48] Numerous countries in Europe traditionally most resistant to such changes are also joining the ranks of the innovators. The dawn of a new era was heralded in France, where English-medium instruction has recently been expanded beyond the elite French business schools and Grandes Ecoles.[49] Scandinavia and the Netherlands have long had a tradition of offering tuition in English at postgraduate level. A different type of regional client is catered for at the Budapest University of Technology and Economics, which has a thriving undergraduate programme taught solely in English[50] that enrols a steady stream of students from Eastern Europe and beyond who can afford Hungary's relatively low course fees while at the same time enjoying high-quality teaching in a country with a rich engineering tradition.

Across the European Union, there is the vast Socrates-Erasmus programme encouraging students from any one country to join a foreign university for up to one year. Participating institutions benefit from this policy-driven mobility scheme by offering courses taught in their region's language or through the medium of English. This has led to speculation that Europe will soon be governed by 'the Erasmus generation' who will be able to network across the continent in a way that was not possible for their forebears, speaking a number of different languages.

However, with some languages as a means of instruction coming under pressure from globalization, many universities are facing a double challenge. They need to find ways of retaining their role of creating intellectual elites in science and for the running of national affairs while at the same time preparing their students for competition in global arenas. Some protection of the home market is afforded through tertiary institutions offering trilingual course programmes. Law students at the Zurich University of Applied Sciences in Winterthur in Switzerland are offered modules in German, French and English, which 'qualify them for a career in business law [in these languages]'.[51] In Italy, the Free University of Bolzano/Bozen has branded itself as a trilingual (Italian, German and English) institution.[52] In these cases, the local multilanguage landscape is exploited to attract students with new products that other universities would struggle to offer.

Other tertiary education institutions are using language incentives to attract students and training professionals alike from across the globe. Long-term investment in learning another language is promoted as an asset and, hence, marketed as a career benefit. The rationale nowadays used in this sector is that the language(s) and cultural know-how alongside technical, legal or other professional skills can boost employability and career prospects. In some Australian universities a language bonus scheme has been introduced to help foster effective participation in a globalized world. For example, the Australian National University has set a benchmark in making language studies compulsory for all students pursuing a bachelor's degree in international business. It also has a language skills component in international security studies to enable 'working with elite international organisations like the United Nations ..., top spy agencies [and to help combat the] threat of military power, civil war, terrorism, cybercrime and environmental degradation'.[53]

Language incentives have also come to form part of post-9/11 US foreign policy. In 2006, the National Security Language Initiative was launched, with President George W. Bush channelling a significant amount of money into the scheme.[54] The strategic aim was to strengthen national security and prosperity through language education. Today, the scheme's stated goal has been reformulated to provide a means of creating essential 'building blocks for citizens to become leaders in a global world'. The programme seeks to attract eligible high school leavers and recent graduates with merit-based scholarships to learn less commonly taught (or 'critical need') languages. This initiative goes alongside a military training programme that offers qualified officers and other enlisted personnel (e.g. doctors and nurses) extra pay for proficiency in languages that are considered of importance to the air force and the navy.[55] US Marines can collect a financial language bonus depending on their skills in, and the number of, additional languages they can offer, and the demand for them. As far as the Foreign Service goes, American diplomats are also expected to become fluent in at least one additional language within the first five years of employment. Proficiency in two other languages is required in order to reach the highest ranks.

In the UK, language and cultural capability has also become associated with national security following the terrorist attacks in London in 2006. The British Army's Language Strategy now includes a 'requirement for all officers to demonstrate a survival level speaking and listening competency in another language in order to be selected for sub-unit command appointments from 2018 onwards'.[56] Such competence is seen as essential 'to communicate effectively and to build a rapport and relationships' while in action. Although no specific languages are currently prescribed, a take-up of Russian and Arabic is recommended for defence interests. Along a similar vein, a recent British Academy report[57] has advanced the idea of phasing in incentives to boost multilingual skills across the British government to avoid the expense of its extensive use of ad hoc contracted interpreters.

To meet the expanding global demand for higher education universities, corporations and cultural institutions have been quick to use the power of digital technology by designing Massive Open Online Courses (MOOCs), the first of which was launched in Canada in 2008. This market is growing rapidly as a new way of recruiting students into a wide range of fields, with computing science and business administration at the forefront. These audio-visual learning platforms have proved popular, with large numbers of students from around the world now following the twelve million already recruited in the United States by Harvard, Stanford and MIT alone. With half of the students coming from developing countries,[58] MOOCs are showing potential as a new model of free and open online learning that democratizes education. This means that anyone around the world with an Internet connection, including those out of education and the socially underprivileged, can benefit from the programmes on offer. Currently, the provider picture is variable. Most MOOCs are stand-alone units, so they are difficult to integrate into the credit-bearing model of university education. In Europe, the development of MOOCs has proceeded at a slower pace than in the United States, with many universities reluctant to accept MOOC credits as contributing towards their own degrees.

The market for MOOCs has so far been mainly through the medium of English (80 per cent), but it is gaining prominence in other languages, particularly in Spanish (8.5 per cent), French (4 per cent) and Chinese (3.5 per cent).[59] MOOCs with a more regional focus have been produced in Germany, Finland, France and Italy. Now, language-specific online platforms (LMOOCs) are also becoming available. *Travailler en français*, co-designed by the UK's Open University and the Institut Français, was the first example dedicated to French language teaching with synchronous sessions focusing on both content and language.[60] With some MOOC units now emerging in partnership with companies (the British retailer Marks and Spencer being one of them[61]), this could widen the market for multilingual collaborations to create employment-specific language training programmes.

This explosion in free online learning environments presents an alternative for students who see their educational prospects curbed by high course fees. MOOCs are also attractive because of their flexibility of access and learning. But they are notorious for their high dropout rate. At any time, there will be those who join for general interest in a given topic, or out of curiosity, but without any sense of commitment. Also, studying using a MOOC proceeds without a physical student community and may lead to student isolation and demotivation. Only a few learners, aiming for certification, will be intent on finishing a module. Among the educational means explored to retain these students are courses that offer blended (regional and global) mechanisms. This combination could, with its support of learning as a social activity, also prove fruitful by adding opportunities for rich and realistic interactions between language students and native speakers.

Universities, striving to reposition themselves in the global marketplace by seeking new education models, are propelling the language revolution in the tertiary sector. As with any other commercial enterprise, their sale of items, designed and repackaged in line with anticipated consumer needs, is likely to proceed along the lines of the commercial slogan

'Your wishes – our command'. But in the education business, students as customers have incomplete knowledge of the product they are setting out to purchase, often as a one-off transaction. What makes a difference to them, and possibly also their sponsors, is the prospect of employability. However, the extent to which the proclaimed language advantage pays dividends is market-dependent. Nevertheless, many tertiary education establishments across the globe are pursuing this market opportunity to increase their student intake by promoting the idea of human capital gains through language skills.

Harnessing mobile resources

When it comes to workforce supply and demand, many advanced industrialized countries seem to be in fortuitous times. People from labour-rich regions such as Mexico are migrating for work to capital-rich ones, such as the United States. With birth rates declining, many advanced economies now depend on cheap labour in a range of industries, particularly agriculture and construction. But migrants need help with both entering and participating in their host labour market. Frequently, perhaps for internal political reasons, languages are used to front divisive debates on immigration. A prevailing argument is that immigrants should not only contribute to the host economy but also integrate linguistically. This is what Sarah Palin alluded to during the 2016 US election campaign when she said on CNN's broadcast 'State of the Union': 'You want to be in America? A), you better be here legally, or you're out of here. B), when you're here, let's speak American. I mean, that's just, that's – let's speak English.'[62]

Various media commentators have suggested that not everyone would agree with the second part of the above statement. Some think that it makes perfect sense to learn the host economy's language but that this will occur naturally while the person is in the country. By implication, many Americans, as former immigrants to a 'New World' that was already inhabited, would have picked up one of their continent's indigenous languages (among them Sioux, Cherokee, Navajo or Mahican), or in the case of the former Governor of Alaska, maybe Inupiaq.

But there are plenty of people who see those taking advantage of the right to free labour movement as a social resource, rather than a problem. Their take on social mobility and the diversity it brings is that it can be advantageous. Naturally, in economic terms, there is a trade-off between costs and benefits of migration. Many migrants need support before they can become economically productive in their host community. Their existing skills may not match demand and they may not be able to speak the language of their host economy where they are trying to become active. This diversity of educational and cultural backgrounds of adult migrants can present a challenge in devising language programmes that are sensitive to their needs.

Building language portfolios

Because migrants have an economic incentive to survive in new environments, they will normally learn their host society's language with commitment and energy. They are aware that this will help them find work. Many, even those with formal qualifications, are known to initially accept a job that is below their skills level, and gradually, as their language proficiency level increases, moving up to posts where communication plays a more central role. A classical example in Europe would be that of a fully qualified surgeon from Bulgaria starting off in a lowly clinical position in Austria, but rising to the post of consultant surgeon on becoming fluent in German. Or the case of a cleaning lady from Slovenia, a qualified accountant, who works her way up in a cleaning company in Italy, resuming her former professional role in their head office. In many cases, public authorities and private bodies employing migrant workers will offer host language instruction, some with incentives (that may result in wage increases).

Governments around the world vary in their approach to integrating economic migrants. With their long-standing tradition of immigration, Canada and Australia have pioneered language integration practices for newcomers. Both governments use a points-based system that is proving popular in the Anglophone sphere, including New Zealand, the UK and Ireland. In this scheme, applicants with high marks for proficiency in the target language and the right qualifications for those domains needed in the labour market have an easier time getting employment or permanent residence. The Citizenship and Immigration Department of Canada runs a well-established language instruction scheme for newcomers that now represents the country's single largest investment in language training. These classes are designed to develop the competencies that newcomers need to function in Canadian society and its economy. The learners' language skills are measured through placement, performance and outcomes tests, and progress is recorded using milestones with credentials in portable language portfolios.[63] This is used to certify an individual's achieved language proficiency level as required for employment, postsecondary study or for gaining immigration status. The system aims to meet the long-term needs of learners, make language training opportunities available to them at the workplace and help them with their personal trajectories and job orientation.

Countries across Europe have now also adopted a range of measures dealing with migration. These are articulated at different policy levels, for entry, temporary or permanent residence, and also for citizenship. Integration programmes that have been set up nationally cover, in many cases, both language and cultural or civil knowledge. In the absence of an EU-wide framework, national procedures vary regarding the language proficiency levels required, the cost, duration and types of courses offered and the methods of assessment.[64] Mostly, in Western Europe (France, Germany, Denmark,

Norway, Luxembourg, Greece), courses and/or language testing are free of charge if they are compulsory to reach a proficiency level set by law. On the other hand, in the Netherlands, Liechtenstein and the UK, costs are currently borne by the migrants themselves. In some cases, monetary incentives are offered based on test results or sanctions applied for not following the required syllabus or failing to take the required language test.

Many people support the idea that governments should implement language examination procedures for newcomers. But in some circles, mainly among language testing professionals, these language-assessment regimes have been variously critiqued regarding their rationale, purpose and consequences. Some experts wonder whether such tests are the best means to measure a newcomer's degree of integration, or conversely, whether these systems serve as an instrument to control migration.[65] Chiefly, the suitability of such language courses will depend on the availability of free and flexible tuition that is relevant to the needs of the learners, supporting them to accomplish tasks in the host language in ways that are appropriate to the changes in their own working life.

Vignette: Educating for work in Denmark

But what is it actually like to attend language classes as a migrant? To conclude this chapter, I shall draw on my own recent experiences. Similar to many other Western European countries, Denmark is experiencing rising levels of immigration. Despite recent changes to the law and campaigns attempting to check this development, over 10 per cent of the Danish population is from other countries. Keeping pace with this trend, Danish language classes are now heavily advertised at the point of arrival to the country, across Copenhagen, in newspapers and on buses. Various types of courses are offered for speakers from different educational, professional and language backgrounds. Tuition is flexible, with intensive classes, e-learning modules or face-to-face tuition supplied by different schools. This is free of charge for persons on the national (CPR) register,[66] as well as for job seekers, a range of professionals (those in business, healthcare or agriculture), higher education students and also for asylum seekers and illiterate individuals. Exams at different levels are required for those applying for permanent residence, for doctors and lawyers, and for those seeking citizenship. According to Danish law, this system is meant to increase employment rates and to enable job seekers to function in a safe society. The proclaimed aim is to avoid ghettos of non-Danish speakers and to discourage dependency on social benefits. Arguably, this social and political instrument is also an expression of some underlying unease nowadays felt throughout Europe about migration. A recent example was in the 2016 debate about UK membership of the European Union, where the 'Leave Campaign' published a list of 50 EU citizens with significant criminal records who had entered the country.[67] In the Danish context, this was graphically illustrated in the Nordic Noir TV series 'The Killing' where one of the chief suspects was a migrant.

However, during my recent lengthy stay in Denmark, I was fascinated to witness how migrants engaged in class with their Danish language work. They were responding vigorously to the high study demands of the course, which was effective, entertaining and relevant to their needs. An audio-visual approach was used in teaching that aimed for functional competence with a work-life focus. Among my coursemates were young engineers from Iran, a project worker from Poland and a medic from Syria. Some of them had escaped from trauma, others had moved between countries (and languages) because of changing labour quotas. They learnt quickly and also spoke a range of other languages, besides perfect English. I saw these people working hard, researching daily in libraries, strategically applying for jobs, integrating into society and eager to contribute to the economy. Motivated to learn the language, they progressed quickly, even with the considerable linguistic distance between Danish and Farsi (for Iranians) or

Arabic (for Syrians) and the different scripts used. They worked
with great intelligence and cognitive ability. My observations of
language classes with illiterate learners revealed similar levels
of engagement. Given a chance, this will bring dividends for
Danish society from the investments made in language classes.

The Danish scenario recognizes that migrants are a
potential resource. Steeped in a democratic tradition of life-
long learning for all, the education system is ready to include
workers from outside. It prepares them for the job market and
also helps foreign entrepreneurs with start-up business plans
to integrate. This taps productively into the resource pool of
people who have come to the country with qualifications,
valuable (entrepreneurial, trading and additional language)
skills and a desire to do well. Reflecting the research by
Chiswick referred to in Chapter 2, this approach recognizes
that investment in incomers' destination language proficiency
is profitable because it enables them to become economically
active and contribute to society.

Returns to migrants and potential benefits for resident
populations can be reasonably expected from learning the
host country's target language. Those intent on settling in
their chosen host society will naturally also benefit from
civic integration programmes for economic and political
participation and, if desired, citizenship, too. However, as
we shall see, many migrants are nowadays more mobile in
responding to multiple short-term employment gaps as they
arise in different countries. This occupational versatility (which
may also include return migration) is producing cosmopolitan
individuals who will benefit from more flexible, workplace-
based language learning practices.

CHAPTER FOUR

Is learning another language worth it?

This chapter comes with a 'health warning', namely that the straightforward question in the title can be answered in different ways, all the way from 'yes, definitely' to 'perhaps' or even 'no'. It all depends on your values. What may be 'worth it' in terms of 'usefulness' or 'importance' might not have any evident material gain. Learning a new language requires a commitment to invest in scarce resources (time and money), in the expectation of some kind of return. A recent podcast discussed this question, in response to the comment below by Doug Ahmann[1]:

> I'm very curious how it came to be that teaching students a foreign language has reached the status it has in the US. My oldest daughter is a college freshman, and not only have I paid for her to study Spanish for the last four or more years [in school] … but her college is requiring her to study even more! … How did it ever get this far? In a day and age where schools at every level are complaining about limited resources, why on earth do we continue to force these kids to study a foreign language that few will ever use, and virtually all do not retain? Or to put it in economics terms, where is the return on investment?

Doug may not have been surprised to learn that the average earnings differential his daughter could expect was, in the words of the podcaster, Stephen Dubner, *only* about 2 per cent. However, as subsequently demonstrated in the *Economist*,[2] the real return on investment of a 2 per cent extra wage is not insignificant over time. Considering a lifetime's earnings, an average 1 per cent salary increase per year and compound interest of a typical university graduate's starting salary of $45,000 turns this bonus over forty years into an extra $67,000 (at 2014 value) that can be added to a pension fund (or retirement account). As we saw in Chapter 2, because of oversupply in the USA, Spanish is the language with the lowest return on investment there, so this sum may well be greater for someone who can offer a language that is high in demand but short in supply.

A cost–benefit calculation on the worth of learning another language might, however, only assess part of the story. It is widely acknowledged that the actual return on such investment can also comprise indirect social or cultural gains. Arguably, Doug's daughter would have ample opportunities to 'retain' her Spanish language skills through interactions with Latino citizens that make up some one-fifth of the overall US population,[3] and with a vast pool of speakers in another nineteen Latin-American countries in South America and more in the Caribbean. Also, she may in time generate more income by drawing inspiration from the richness of Hispanic cultures.

Market incentives

Facebook's founder Mark Zuckerberg is one of those for whom knowledge of another language has both personal and professional worth. He is quoted as saying: 'There are three reasons I decided to learn Chinese. The first, my wife is Chinese. Her grandmother can only speak Chinese. When I told her in Chinese I was going to marry Priscilla, she was very shocked. Then I want to study Chinese culture. The third: Chinese is hard and I like a challenge.'[4] He also has a market-driven incentive for acquiring ability in the language as this may in due course yield material benefits flowing from China into his company. In an article entitled 'Mark Zuckerberg Courts China With Speech on People and Perseverance', it is suggested that this entrepreneur's deployment of Mandarin at Tsinghua University in Beijing (where he is on the advisory board) is a 'calculated move to appeal to Chinese users'.[5]

Like Twitter, YouTube and other social media platforms, Facebook has been blocked in China since 2009. Its creator is driven by enormous financial incentives to connect another billion users (roughly the equivalent of China's population) with the rest of the world using his platform. In trying to penetrate the Chinese market by speaking their language, he follows an old mantra that was most famously expressed by Willy Brandt, the former Chancellor of the Federal Republic of Germany: 'If I'm selling to you, I speak your language. But if I'm buying, dann müssen Sie Deutsch sprechen [then you have to speak German].' In other words, sales are more likely when consumers can get information about a product or service in their own language. This approach is not new. The ancient traders we followed earlier in this book knew that they could increase their sales by using the language of their customers.

A recent Economist Intelligence Unit report on how cultural and language barriers affect business confirms that effective cross-border communication and collaboration are critical for the financial success of companies with international aspirations.[6] Executives interviewed from across the world stated that better communication with customers and colleagues abroad benefits their company's profit, revenue and market share. In fact, around half of the respondents admit that misunderstandings have stood in the way of major cross-border transactions, incurring significant losses for their company.[7] These findings suggest that, to mitigate the corporations' risks of language gaps affecting their financial performance, greater investment in language and communication training and better recruitment and selection procedures are necessary. The implication is that international companies have strong economic incentives to ensure that their approach is in line with corporate strategies and goals.

Findings in the above survey also confirm that successful communication in an international environment depends not only on the ability to speak various languages but also to handle cultural differences. Entrepreneurs attempting to break into a new market know that they need to conduct their negotiations in a culturally sensitive way. It was such awareness that enabled Egyptian entrepreneur Samih Sawiris to win approval in order to build the largest ever ski project in the Swiss Alps, in Andermatt. To achieve this, he needed to negotiate with government officials for an exemption from property buying regulations that control foreign real estate ownership in Switzerland. In 'Bankrolling a new Swiss resort',[8] the billionaire backer is quoted as saying that in his business he uses a 'multi-pronged approach of investment, attracting the right buyers and keeping locals involved'. In a country such as Switzerland that is known for its consensus-based democracy, this is a gargantuan task. His success with this venture shows his ability to build trust and a good rapport convincingly in German, a language he had learnt when he was at University in Berlin. In his case, the ROI is likely to be far greater than that predicted for Doug's daughter.

Clearly, deployment of intercultural competence demands emotional intelligence and finely tuned language skills to pay dividends. As Richard Hardie, Chairman of the investment bank UBS, puts it: 'A deep understanding of foreign languages is often essential to the combination of cajolery and seduction many companies require in their international negotiations.' However, he stresses that businesses need graduates with more than conversation skills and a good technical vocabulary. The really valuable negotiators, in his eyes, are those able to produce subtle phrasing to 'persuade someone from another culture to do something they would not otherwise want to do',[9] suggesting a need for people who are not just 'book-smart' but also 'street-smart'. It is perhaps no surprise that the ten most favoured critical soft skills pursued by recruiters and headhunters include cross-cultural competency and communication.[10] These are considered as central in a fast-changing and complex world that brings people together from diverse cultures.

In response to the needs of employers, leading institutions offering MBA degrees, such as the London Business School or the Thunderbird School of Global Management (the oldest and largest graduate school for international business in the United States), have stand-alone programmes where cross-cultural training is embedded in language learning. These focus on the types of negotiations employees might undertake, the decisions they will face, the social events in which they might participate and the wide variation in behaviours and preferences in different cultures. Emphasis is also placed on how to handle the fundamentals of both verbal and non-verbal communication in international environments and on how to ensure that body language (facial expressions, a particular hand motion or even silence) does not convey unintended messages in cross-cultural encounters. Equipping students with soft skills is seen as a form of personal development and is meant to aid their employability. In the words of Mohammed Khalid, a graduate from Hult International Business School, this distinctive skills set has real value for an employer: 'It's about how others perceive you, which is not always the way you think. ... There was a huge emphasis on integrity, and working on these soft skills helped me get the position of sales account manager.'[11]

The ability to work constructively with an understanding that culture influences the way you think about things is seen as a valuable asset for employees at all corporate levels. This much-sought-after skill is essential whether for the preparation of export marketing strategies or for the management of international subsidiaries with a culturally diverse workforce. In fact, research carried out over the last decade in the United States on language in global organizations and teams suggests that even when group members are fluent in a lingua franca, a lack of cultural awareness can cause significant misunderstandings and disagreements, masking divergent group norms, practices and expectations.[12] Consider a business meeting in Stockholm with executives from the United States and Japan. With the predominance of Westerners present, there may be an expectation for communication to be direct and to the point. But this might clash with the oriental mindset, which is less inclined to address a topic head on. The Japanese Mitsubishi representative may well prefer to answer a question with a 'maybe' or 'we'll see' rather than a 'no', in order to save face. Is he delaying the progress of negotiations or should his Swedish and US counterparts address his cultural needs more sensitively? On this question rests the state of their professional relationships. A recent survey on culture at work has revealed that many human resource managers of large companies from across the world operate with the awareness that culture impacts business. Findings indicate that they regard intercultural sensitivity as a core soft skill that benefits their organization in terms of bringing in new clients, reduces team conflict and supports their organization's reputation.[13]

Greater employment opportunities are likely for those who can offer a telling combination of soft (transferable) and hard (technical) skills in a field, such as perhaps economics, engineering or law. However, such personal attributes are no guarantee of employment since the demand for them is subject to the usual market forces. High demand but low supply results in employment opportunities whereas a low demand but ample supply means job scarcity. Some multilingual employees may only reap dividends later when they are sent abroad some years into the job. Or they may seize a chance to deploy their native language expertise in a region of high demand. Kate demonstrates her success with this strategy in the blog entry below that came in reply to this chapter's introductory posting by Doug[14]:

I spent two years unsuccessfully looking for a job in the US after graduating in 2011 (not even a business degree and two foreign languages could help me find anything other than a minimum-wage internship). However, last year I decided to move to a Latin American country currently experiencing much more economic growth than the US and use my Spanish fluency in my job search. Upon arriving I immediately got hired by one of the biggest and most highly esteemed tech companies in the world – one of the very same companies that didn't even give my resume the time of day back in the States. Since finding such success down south many of my unemployed friends back home have mentioned wanting to follow in my footsteps – the only problem is they don't speak a second language.

For her, the benefit of learning an additional language was that this opened up other options. It gave her the flexibility to look for job opportunities abroad and move to a country whose economy is growing faster than her own. She found her comparative language advantage not as an incidental speaker in the crowded Spanish language market of the United States, but as a native English speaker in Latin America who could also work in Spanish. This proficiency in a second language and her international work experience would likely translate to higher wages over her career. In addition, having extended her networks into another culture, she might in due course also derive a range of other social and personal benefits.

Language beliefs

So far in this book, we have seen plenty of evidence that multilingualism can benefit both individuals and society. Knowing more than one language expands our knowledge, opens up opportunities and even boosts employability. And yet, in spite of the fact that we can derive a range of advantages from learning languages, many people choose not to do so. What are their reasons and what case can be made for language study?

Myths and facts

'I am no good at learning other languages.'

This comment can only come from someone who has never needed to learn another language. We all have proved early in life that we have a natural ability to acquire language. An unwillingness to make further language investments subsequently displays a lack of motivation, not incapacity. Admittedly, a bad learning experience, half-hearted attempts or unrealistic expectations can be temporary stumbling blocks along the way. When linked with the popular myth that some people have a special language talent, such setbacks may well become a self-fulfilling prophecy. But there is no such thing as a language-learning gene. Individuals like Cleopatra or Marco Polo (among many others) used languages as a means to their ends, and hence made an effort to acquire the skills they needed.

It does perhaps not help that occasionally some particularly multilingual individuals are popularized as polyglots, or even 'hyperglots'. One such example is the legendary Cardinal Mezzofanti, a nineteenth-century priest in Italy, who reputedly knew some seventy-two languages.[15] Language systems will have resonated well with him, but mainly he will have enjoyed the process of learning, as is the case with musicians when rehearsing. However, as with being able to 'play' an instrument, 'knowing' a language means different things to different people. More normally, people will add to their language repertoires as they go along, without any grandiose ambitions. For many, an ability to conduct daily face-to-face communication is sufficient; others will strive for higher-level language mastery. The worth of both ends of the proficiency spectrum to us depends on our aspirations and resources.

'I am too old to learn another language.'

It is true that language acquisition by young children is different from that by adults. Children do so spontaneously but need more time. However, later on in life, given a positive attitude and passion about what we are setting out to do, we become, in many ways, better learners. We develop learning strategies and work with our ability to transfer knowledge. If focused on a specific goal, we can set milestones to hone our progress and consolidate our achievements. Furthermore, as we shall see below, the acrobatics of learning another language can, in fact, stimulate our brains.

Admittedly, a 'native-like' competence in another language is harder to achieve after childhood. But this should not deter anyone from broadening their cultural horizon. Equal dual language ability is more an ideal than actually achieved in practice. Many of us have linguistic fortes and foibles, even in the language(s) we use most often. Naturally, our familiarity with any language we know is linked to our personal biographies and the nature of our engagement in the various language communities we have lived in. As far as a native French speaker's multilingual repertoire goes, this may be fairly evenly developed in say, Japanese, partially exist in Russian, with a more basic proficiency level in English. All of these language fragments, whether used singly or even by switching from one to another, can serve to make communication happen in different multilingual encounters. Awareness of how to best exploit our own language resources can certainly be productive.

'I don't want to lose my own language.'

This is a wild card. The fear of losing one's native tongue when learning another language is unfounded. But there is evidence that this possibility was already considered during the era of discovery. John Hunter, one of James Cook's companions, wrote in his journal on board the Sirius during a voyage to New South Wales on 20 January 1788: '[The] Governor is desirous of having a Man or two in our possession to whom we might teach enough of our Language without the danger of losing any part of their own, to render them usefull to their

Countrymen.'[16] The practical concern then was that indigenous individuals ('a Man or two') needed to be able to retain their own language if they were to act as messengers between the explorers and their own community.

We know nowadays that people's language ability may, indeed, falter over a lifespan, though this is rare and mainly occurs following trauma. In general, as far as reduced language faculty is concerned, this has been linked to a mutation of the brain gene FOXP2 that was discovered a decade ago. Of course, an individual's primary language skills may atrophy somewhat on settling in another language area, especially if this happens at an early age. But the mother tongue is not normally lost if it has been used continuously into adulthood. So, if you have moved your mountaineering business from the Himalayas to the Andes, you should normally still be able to retrieve your first language (perhaps Sherpa or Nepali) comfortably decades later in your adopted Spanish- (or Quechua) speaking language environment. But if you were born in Bangkok and then moved to Teheran as a toddler, you may not retain your native Thai language if your parents are not using it with you.

'I can get instant translations anywhere when I need it.'

It is, indeed, the case that translation technologies are offering *one* solution to bridging some language divides. We had evidence of this from the hospital ward round account in Chapter 3. Google's famous translation engine currently covers ninety languages, formerly mainly European ones, but now stretching wider, from Afrikaans to Khmer and Zulu. Microsoft Skype translator supports seven languages (Chinese, English, French, German, Italian, Portuguese and Spanish) for voice/video calls and fifty languages for instant messaging.[17] Facebook now has well over a hundred languages, and Twitter more than fifty. These tools play a key role in connecting ever more diverse language communities across the globe. Arguably, the range of languages covered is still not enough, and billions of people are digitally disenfranchised.

This is illustrated by the story of an acquaintance, who works in London with homeless refugees from all over the world. She often needs to use Google Translate and says that this can be a valuable tool if you talk a language that is popular (especially in business), for example Arabic. But she regrets that no instant resource is available when requiring translating into, for example, Amharic or Tigrinya. These are large language groups (with twenty-two million and seven million speakers, respectively) that are, however, not represented on Google. And yet these languages are currently much in demand, with millions of people escaping from poverty, persecution and human rights abuses in Ethiopia and Eritrea.[18]

'Why bother, since everyone speaks English anyway.'

Is it really the case that monolingual English speakers do not have to learn another language because everyone else knows theirs? This claim can hardly be substantiated when you consider the homeless refugees mentioned above. In fact, it is estimated that two-thirds of the world's population cannot speak English[19] at all. What is more, of those who can, the vast majority (well over 80 per cent) do so as their second language – and in terms of its position as a world language, English is ranked fourth (after Mandarin Chinese, Spanish and Hindi).

These figures show that English is not the universal lingua franca as is often assumed. So why do people think that everyone can speak English? For sure it has gained prominence as the language of countries that have been at the forefront of globalization. And nowadays, it is true that wherever you go, you are likely to meet someone who knows *some* English. But unless they stick to well-trodden (tourist) paths and hope to depend on 'the kindness of strangers', monolingual English speakers risk losing out to those who are better equipped to take advantage of their lack of linguistic abilities. Clearly, instant translation tools can only give rudimentary assistance.

Such myths aside, languages clearly matter because they provide access to specific resources (e.g. information, knowledge, water, food or medical treatment). Learning another language is an effort we may have to make for practical reasons, perhaps to move abroad or to satisfy citizenship requirements in another country where we want to settle. Some of us decide to learn a new language in response to an economic prompt. Others may be driven by curiosity or a desire to break down communication barriers with people from other cultures. Or else they may be propelled by pure interest in a particular language or a wish to gain access to a culture they are passionate about. This could be a desire to be able to read original manga in Japanese, to cook using original French recipes or to explore the Goths' subculture in a Scandinavian language. Many more cases can be made for learning another language, sometimes allowing for unexpected benefits. There are stories about individuals who are doing so to combat loneliness, to beat depression, to shed inhibitions or to discover the dormant actor within.

Other pay-offs

We sometimes come across headlines suggesting that bilinguals 'are smarter',[20] that they 'have more grey matter than monolinguals',[21] and that 'being bilingual may delay Alzheimer's and boost brain power'.[22] It has even been claimed that 'thinking in a foreign language makes decisions more rational'.[23] What are the facts behind these assertions?

There is growing evidence that people can derive cognitive benefits from second language study, at any age.[24] More specifically, research points to bilinguals ending up with improved attention, intelligence and better verbal and spatial abilities.[25] Hypothetically, this relates to an increased capacity for individuals to process information, likely as a result of structural changes in the networks and connections of the brain. This is thought to happen because, like any brain games, logic or visual exercises, language learning can stimulate and alter the structure of the brain in the same way that a person can build muscle mass. This process, called neuroplasticity, means that our brain changes through experience.

Thus, individuals who learn a second language can be seen to have, overall, better mental skills. What has been observed in a series of experiments on more than three hundred people from the United States and Korea is that using a second language eliminates their tendency towards loss aversion and, hence, reduces decision-making biases that unduly influence how risks and benefits are perceived. The proposition is that this happens because speaking an additional language provides greater cognitive and emotional understanding than would be the case with the use of just the native tongue.[26] This might well help improve an individual's ability to make better financial choices. Of particular interest here is the fact that neuroscience is beginning to show that bilingual people may have attributes that are highly valued in employment: analytical thinking, conceptualizing ability, working memory and dexterity. These skills are assets when it comes to rational planning, managing complexity and problem-solving, which are central for executive function.

Furthermore, some people derive emotional benefits from different languages. For example, it is not uncommon for individuals to connect particular languages with certain qualities and, hence, get pleasure from using them. Some might find Italian melodious, French beautiful and German logical. Others might learn Italian for opera, French for haute couture and German for philosophy. Arguably, our attitudes towards particular languages are largely shaped by where we live and the experiences we have by way of upbringing, travel and events.

The following anecdote from the sixteenth century is perhaps a tongue-in-cheek illustration of an individual who, we might say, simultaneously lived and used languages. The person in question, Charles V, headed an almost universal monarchy in Europe. He came from the House of Habsburg, was Duke of Burgundy, ruled over the Netherlands and the Spanish Empire as well as Italy and Germany as Holy Roman Emperor. He had six children by his wife Isabella of Portugal and four more offspring in Austria. Notably, he also knew several languages, as did many people in his time. The story goes that:

> if it was necessary to talk with God, he would talk in Spanish, which language suggests itself for the graveness and majesty of the Spaniards; if with friends, in Italian, for the dialect of the Italians was one of familiarity; if to caress someone, in French, for no language is tenderer than theirs; if to threaten someone or to speak harshly to them, in German, for their entire language is threatening, rough and vehement.[27]

We may not agree with his take on languages, and there are several versions of what he supposedly said. But this multilingual ruler firmly planted the idea that languages have qualities and fit a purpose. For him, Spanish was the medium of religious protocol and French, his native tongue, had emotional depth. His knowledge of these two Romance languages would explain his familiarity with Italian. He likely used German to rule over his German-speaking subjects, who had split loyalties.

We get the impression that Charles V was not just a multilingual ruler. Rather, he had a passion about being multilingual and expressed his emotions through the languages he knew. This affective dimension of multilingualism for speakers who use two or more languages in their everyday lives is now well documented.[28] It is exploited in marketing, as in the slogan 'Vorsprung durch Technik' that evokes associations with quality, reliability and innovation.

Language choices

A recent British Council report has identified Spanish, Arabic, French, Mandarin Chinese, German, Portuguese, Italian, Russian, Turkish and Japanese as the languages for the future, besides English.[29] This list is based mainly on economic, geopolitical, cultural and educational grounds, including prevalence on the Internet. The prediction is that these languages will be the most major ones the UK will need for building international relationships over the coming decades, particularly regarding trading opportunities and market growth. It comes in response to government statistics that show that the UK loses about 3.5 per cent of GDP (that is about £50 billion) every year as a result of a lack of language skills in the workforce.[30] This contrasts with the annual gains of 9 per cent made in Switzerland through multilingualism.

But this choice of priority languages hardly comes as a surprise, and readily applies to other countries, too. Knowledge of (modern standard) Arabic is key for those in the petroleum industry. Although the language is widespread with over three hundred million users worldwide, it has relatively few speakers in the West. German, too, would seem a safe investment, with Germany figuring as the number one economy in Europe and the world's second largest exporter. Spoken by some 101 million people worldwide and also used as a lingua franca in parts of Central and Eastern Europe, it is a language that many employers in engineering and in the pharmaceutical industry will want their workforce to be familiar with. Unlike Arabic, it is not an official UN language, but it is a key one in the European Union. Spanish, with some five hundred million speakers on both sides of the Atlantic and as the predominant language of Latin America's fast-growing economies, naturally features highly among managers' preferences. Clearly, this is the one language where the United States has the domestic advantage of a sizeable bilingual Hispanic resource pool, with many occupying positions in sales, marketing or healthcare. French, the language of over

220 million people in forty countries, has currency across all continents and is forecast to grow in several of the world's fast-developing markets, particularly in sub-Saharan Africa. It has also some cachet with its sector-specific wine export tradition, and it is an official language in many international institutions including the United Nations, the European Union, in two of the G8 group of industrialized nations[31] and in the International Olympics Committee (itself founded by a Frenchman). Furthermore, with the rapidly growing BRIC economies that represent some two-fifths of the world's population, the demand for Mandarin and Portuguese is firmly set on the global market, alongside Russian. What is more, entrepreneurs in the hi-tech industry depend heavily on employees skilled in Mandarin and Japanese. So the British Council would appear to have got it right. But why is Turkish on the list? As a language spoken by over sixty-five million people in southeastern Europe, Western Asia and across parts of the European Union this is an emerging high-growth market. It is also sought after for geopolitical reasons, alongside Farsi and Arabic.

How do we respond to these diverse drivers? We all rise to the bait of different incentives in the choices we make. In our decisions about languages, our personal interests and professional ambitions guide us, whether in exports, security, teaching or translating. To some extent, the language investment options individuals are prepared to engage in reflect their risk profile. A risk-taker may well embark on studying Turkish as one of the proclaimed languages for the future. Another approach would be to 'play it safe', aiming strictly for proven rather than hoped-for income potential. So someone else, a translator for example, might work better from and into a language she feels connected to for some reason, maybe through marriage or travel. She might struggle with the prospect of dealing with a language that is culturally distant or that has a different script. In choosing a language that reflects her deeper affinity with a culture she may well reap material and personal benefits. Clearly, knowledge of English is implicitly assumed nowadays for anyone in business, research or tourism. But since it already has a large supply of speakers, it may be less suited for those with an eye to tapping into specific niche markets.

From a purely utilitarian perspective, a rational decision on the merits of one language option over another is concerned with the economic advantages this brings. Choosing a language that is considered high in demand but short in supply in a given region would be a viable strategy for those focused on income maximization. In proactively matching this balance, an individual may well experience an increase in his or her earnings. Just like elsewhere in the market, investing in a resource that is scarce yields more benefits and profits. For example, translators in the European Union who are able to offer one of the newer accession languages (for example, Hungarian, Bulgarian or Maltese),[32] in addition to the more standard Western European choices, can expect to be in demand. Conversely, those working in a saturated market, as is the case in the United States with Anglophone translators into Spanish, might fare better in considering moving their specialism or geographic remit of work.

Whatever our actual drivers, the language decisions we make reflect, to some extent, how we like to position ourselves in the world. Ultimately, a multilingual individual's productivity will be linked to a myriad of factors, largely chance, flexibility and also an ability to seize opportunities. The effort required largely depends on the types of language skills and level of proficiency aimed at. Some learners work better in an organized class-based setting whereas others prefer a flexible, informal approach. Steady progress is more likely by combining both types of learning styles.

Approaches to learning

What type of a learner are you? Some of us use a slow and deliberate pace. Others prefer to move on swiftly. Perhaps you belong to the latter group? If so, and supposing you are interested in learning another language, you might well respond to the proposition that you can get 'from zero to fluency' in just three months, whatever your age.[33] 'Speak from day one, learn fast' is what Benny Lewis, a vociferous promoter of the 'swift method', recommends. He takes a no-nonsense 'you can do it' approach to language learning, calling for determination and a preparedness to put in plenty of practice and time. Achieving 'fluency' in another language should indeed be feasible within three months if it is understood as a functional ability to deal with everyday situations such as ordering food, making a hotel reservation or locating a train station. It seems that Lewis's published toolkit struck a chord with businesses and individuals alike, topping ranking lists on Amazon in the United States, Canada and the United Kingdom.

This interest suggests that many people in Anglophone countries would like to learn another language. In particular, it appears that the idea of doing so fast has appeal. A concentrated start is certainly optimal for acquiring the fundamentals of any new skill. However, not everyone is able to release sufficient time and energy for accelerated study. Those in employment, for example, need to be able to do so flexibly; others work better if they can combine learning with entertainment. They certainly can, with plenty of freely available online learning tools. Among them is Duolingo, which offers learning that is 'fun, easy, and scientifically proven'.[34] Its Guatemalan creator, Luis von Ahn, had the idea 'to develop an educational opportunity so that those without much money could learn a language, advance their chances of getting a job and increase their income potential'.[35] Clearly, not everyone needs this type of incentive. Microsoft's monolingual billionaire Bill Gates was quoted as saying that he 'gave up [Duolingo] without a reason'.[36] Such 'dipping in and out' offers a taste of learning something new but is a well-known by-product of online learning, as we saw in the case of MOOCS.

These online tools 'do what they say on the tin'. Social media, apps and websites such as YouTube are clearly driving language-learning productivity. With a wealth of immersive platforms, they offer structured study for many languages to suit a variety of tastes and needs. The environments they provide are meant to be enjoyable and informative, which can make learning more effective. Available in an ever-increasing range of languages, this massive resource with its multiplicity of uses coalesces with suites of online chat rooms,[37] initiating novices to a language. Frequent and regular exposure is particularly valuable where a language is significantly different from that of the learner. For example, a Westerner battling with the intricate intonation pattern of Mandarin could do worse than occasionally 'chatting' online with native speakers. Such experience-based learning can, indeed, support the process of language acquisition from the beginner to the advanced level, but is likely to work better in combination with deliberate practice.

But, overall, the progress we make when learning a language is not as much about the tools chosen as the method and focus applied. Online and offline study, apps or books all have their place, whether in organized or informal settings, and depending on their availability and particular objectives. In many ways, the latest technology, increasingly personal and contextual, has fundamentally changed the relationship between individuals and their (language) learning experience. Wearable and companionable, many devices offer on the spot 'personal assistance' and, hence, have considerable utility potential as they become ever more integrated with everyday life. Mobile and flexible learning appeals because it enables 'on-the-go' progression. With active and frequent engagement possible anytime and anywhere, second language use has perhaps become easier.

It almost seems that we can learn a new language by osmosis nowadays. Through instant translation engines, the world is literally at your fingertips. But these powerful aids are rudimentary tools and, hence, have to be used judiciously. They are no perfect language solution. Engaging more deeply with another language is a cognitive process and therefore requires time. In many ways, it is an ongoing journey of development, interaction and discovery.

Language levels

An American civil servant is studying Arabic for a posting in Baghdad. A Polish barber is learning Croatian to run a business in Zagreb. An Austrian healthcare worker is trying to pick up skills in Yoruba for a polio eradication assignment in Nigeria. All of them are navigating their way through a language system that is new to them. They are focused on their various goals, and their proficiency is increasing incrementally. When do they know enough of their target language to be able to use it in their new work place? There is no simple answer to this question since different skills are required in each case. The embassy worker will benefit from some familiarity with the Arabic (abjad) writing system to function in Iraq; the shop owner needs colloquial language skills; the project nurse requires health-related vocabulary.

These examples show that 'knowing' another language is a vague concept. It may be seen as a single competence that varies individually in terms of fluency, extent and depth of use. More commonly, nowadays language proficiency is understood as a set of skills that can be measured according to international standards. Widely adopted today is the Common European Framework of Reference for Languages (CEFR). This provides a comprehensive and transparent system to define a learner's language ability. An assessment grid[38] is used to categorize what a student should be able to do in listening, speaking, reading and writing at three pairs of language levels ranging from basic (A1/2) to intermediate (B1/2) and proficient (C1/2). For example, in speaking, a learner is expected to demonstrate at the basic level an ability to exchange simple information (e.g. asking questions about a menu), at the intermediate level a capacity to deal with more general information (e.g. opening a bank account), and at the proficient level the faculty of processing cognitively demanding information to good effect (e.g. discussing the pros and cons of migration).

The CEFR scheme makes it possible to give differentiated descriptions of someone's language skills as may be required for foreign job applicants or university entrants. Currently, in Germany for example, a medical doctor from another country should have general language competence at level B2 (corresponding to good average proficiency, according to the CEFR), whereas his or her medical language skills should be more advanced, at level C1 of the CEFR. The official requirement in Germany is that an incomer's language proficiency level should be proved in dedicated tests under the responsibility of the area health authorities.[39] Many countries nowadays use some kind of language screening as a condition for cross-border employment.[40] This is to ensure working language competencies at appropriate levels across different occupations.

Where multilanguage skills are a job requirement in the domestic employment sector, a basic proficiency will rarely be regarded as sufficient. The use of the term 'fluency' in recruitment tends to imply a standard beyond higher education entrance level, at which point an employee is normally expected to be able to perform work assignments in that language. More commonly, this needs to be at a general, advanced or more specific business level. Employers know that an ability to confidently, say, negotiate a wine import deal using French with the correct tone is likely to pay dividends since no amount of translation can be as effective or persuasive as face-to-face communication. This is especially the case before signing a contract, when being able to interact effectively in the language of a trade partner counts. Quite apart from understanding technical references, a joke, a pun or tiny nuances that may easily get lost in translation could eventually turn out to matter. However, while multilingual skills are important, they are by no means the only requirement in intercultural communication. Anyone engaging with people from various language backgrounds also needs an awareness of how cultural differences can affect social relationships and outcomes. This is where soft skills come in, as discussed before. Headhunters will, therefore, want to recruit people with the cultural know-how to deal effectively with colleagues and clients abroad. Job candidates able to demonstrate their language agility and cultural astuteness in interviews that may be conducted by switching between languages will find that their chances of being hired are enhanced.

Employment prospects

Anyone currently searching for employment in investment banking might encounter the headline: 'Speaking another language can help you get a graduate investment banking job'.[41] With the fierce competition nowadays to find a position in banking, graduates with skills in another language might stand out among co-applicants. Job seekers able to offer technical expertise, for example in IT, law, finance or sales, combined with relevant language skills will find themselves in greater demand. Some of the major players in the industry are looking for experts in a wide range of languages: Barclays Wealth needs Arabic, Mandarin, Hindi, French and Spanish; Nomura wants Spanish, Italian, French, German, Dutch, Swedish, Norwegian and Russian; Goldman Sachs has vacancies for French, Russian, German, Italian and Spanish speakers. These are the requirements now; the array of desired languages might change in line with business developments in growth markets, such as Turkey and Russia. Some companies require specific languages for a few roles only (Bank of America), some for overseas opportunities in sales and investment banking (Barclays Capital), while other firms are developing a genuine multiple language profile. Goldman Sachs, among many others, is seeking language graduates or native speakers for around 50 per cent of their roles as merchant bankers,[42] particularly in their client-facing divisions. Similarly, many other companies use a deliberate hiring and training strategy in the knowledge that they can, as was also echoed recently in the Harvard Business Review, turn language into a source of competitiveness[43] in driving consumer behaviour, market share and brand preference.

Candidates selected for such appointments are normally required to have advanced ability in a second language. Or else they are bilingual speakers who, like Kate earlier on in this chapter, accept a position abroad where their native language is in demand. Employers like Kate's are increasingly turning to the international job market in their recruitment of suitable candidates to fill existing skills gaps. But some regions in need of technical know-how have been reported to be experiencing an undersupply of experts able to take on key positions to fill the gap. Across Asia, in China and Hong Kong for example, banks want (Western) experts with relevant language skills for middle to senior management positions, particularly in investment banking, governance, risk control and compliance, and also for hi-tech jobs.[44] However, the high-level local language capability that would be required for such positions is often found to be in short supply among Westerners, whose skills and experience in technical areas such as options trading and broking are in great demand. In the West too, with the growing importance of the Middle East in international affairs, there is a shortage of experts versed in Arabic to fill posts in many areas of business and industry, finance, banking and consulting. Additionally, governments need similar expertise in their overseas and intelligence services. A recent survey in Australia has confirmed that learning another (culturally distant, Indonesian or Asian) language has benefitted career prospects abroad for numerous engineers, lawyers, consultants, journalists and those in advertising and logistics, in addition to teachers and interpreters. The author of the study (Jeff Neilson, a geographer at the University of Sydney) has himself experienced the added value of knowing another language, and says that on door-knocking employers in Jakarta, he found himself being hired by a global consulting firm there.[45]

The demand for language specialists at the corporate level is mirrored in the public sector. Prompted by greater language requirements through cross-border mobility, many governments around the world are adjusting their social policy. There is a need to ensure language provision and access to information across all sections of society. This is particularly the case in the civil service, in healthcare, and in the economic and other social spheres. As a consequence, there is a greater reliance on language services for the provision of information in multiple language formats for clients from different cultural backgrounds. But supplying interpreting in a particular language as may be required in courtrooms, hospitals and for housing can, as we have seen, be challenging. In many places where there is a great language need, it cannot always be met by supply. Indeed, some regions of the world are struggling to provide adequate language infrastructure for their population. An example is Canada's Northwest Territories with eleven official languages,[46] where employers are registering a large number of unfilled vacancies because of the shortage of language skills in the workforce. To attract more people to the various language regions, local authorities are now offering applicants able to work in a language other than English a bilingual wage bonus. This skill is seen as essential to provide adequate public service in the various district communities across a whole range of positions and at all professional levels, from law to health and education.

An ever-growing range of opportunities for language professionals also exists within the expanding European Union. About 1 per cent of its annual general budget is spent on employing linguists and support staff to operate one of the largest translation services in the world.[47] Added to this are numerous opportunities in response to the European Parliament's call on national broadcasting authorities to include translation (or subtitles) of television news programmes into sign language. Language provisions enabling accessibility to services for sign- and regional-language users (who amount to about one-tenth of the total EU population) are also expected at a national level. Moreover, member states are urged to supply public signs in Braille for the benefit of blind people or those with impaired vision. Special language facilities exist in officially bilingual cities such as Bruxelles/Brussels (with French and Dutch) and Bolzano/Bozen in South Tyrol (with Italian and German), or in regions such as Prekmurje in Slovenia (with Slovenian and Hungarian). Here, the media, official information and documents are usually handled bilingually. In general, translation work in public administration tends to be outsourced to freelancers and agencies. As a result of this wide-ranging demand for language services, different types of language provider enterprises now exist that offer translation and other specialist services and courses such as corporate sign-language training.[48]

There is also a growing virtual marketplace that aims to put language service specialists in contact with prospective clients. One such enterprise is Galilea3, which describes itself as a multilingual marketplace where freelancers can post their services in various languages (currently English, Spanish, Russian, French, German, Arabic and Polish). Aiming to 'increase the global reach of both sellers and buyers of services by eliminating language barriers', this company's two co-founders describe themselves as 'holders of master's degrees in technical fields not related to web development, but hav[ing] always had a passion for all things IT related'.[49]

Overall, it is now well established that people with multilingual skills and interest in different cultures, technological development and global business will find themselves in demand, be it for employment in teaching, translation, tourism, trade, PR, communications and management or government service. The range of opportunities for language specialists is likely to continue to expand as teams of linguists, scientists, developers, designers, teachers, communication experts and others from different countries collaborate in today's globalized world. This widening need, together with the associated supporting services, will mean that employment opportunities for multilingual individuals will increase in the foreseeable future.

CHAPTER FIVE

Languages in the marketplace

It was a late January night when I travelled from Copenhagen across the Øresund Bridge to Malmö. I was tired and hungry and the restaurant was about to close. But I was given a warm welcome and ten minutes later found myself digging into a delicious fish pie. The waiter, in his late twenties, was from Romania. He had started working in Sweden just that week. Previously, he had been in France, Italy and Germany. When he talked, he switched between languages that he had picked up from these different hosting communities. He was planning to stay in Malmö over the summer season so that he could also add some Swedish to his repertoire of languages.

This smart young man was already starting to contribute to his newly adopted country's economy even though he knew only a few words of Swedish. He had found employment in this restaurant because his other languages enabled him to talk to a variety of customers. His combined language repertoire was functional, focused on his task as a waiter. Not intent on settling down just yet, he may in due course decide to move on to a different country or return to one where he had lived previously. Or else, like many other migrants, he may decide to return to his native country where his partial knowledge of different languages might serve him in setting up his own business or finding employment. For him, and others, too, cross-border migration is not necessarily a lifetime decision but, rather, a flexible period in response to employment opportunities. With people routinely moving abroad for work, encounters such as the one above between polyglot individuals have become an everyday phenomenon for many, particularly in urban areas.

Language repertoires of this type are not specific to migrants. Many of us are potentially or actually multilingual, to various degrees. We study different languages formally or acquire them casually in our families, at work or when we travel. Others learn languages specific to certain professional domains, for example engineering, gastronomy or nursing. An individual's level of competence in different languages will vary, and it will change over a lifetime. None of these proficiencies may ever equal a native speaker's ability or even involve literacy, as may be the case with our Romanian waiter above. But all the language snippets we pick up as we go along can be used for action, singly or as an amalgamated repertoire. Indeed, such multilingual competencies may have economic potential in culturally diverse contexts.

Multilingual workplace practices

An ability to function flexibly across languages and cultures has currency in the international marketplace. As many global businesses readily show on their websites, they value a culturally diverse talent pool in their workforce. Among the reasons voiced by companies are that this helps 'to remain competitive…, understand the markets [they] serve … and solve [their] clients' problems' (IBM),[1] and that 'such a combination of cultures creates [a] mix of ideas, vision and knowledge' (Airbus).[2]

Clearly, multilingual employees are needed for international negotiations, assignments, mergers and acquisitions. The corporate idea is that effective leveraging of a strategically recruited talent pool drives creativity to secure a competitive edge. In a recent survey carried out by the *Economist,* some two-thirds of 572 international company executives[3] confirm that the multicultural nature of teams within their company increases innovation. In fact, Michelin, proclaiming a 'passion for innovation' as its central strategy, organizes in-house challenges called 'InnovationWorks', where employees from China, the United States and Europe are drawn together to share their ideas. Some teams are then selected to join the Michelin 'incubator'.[4]

On-site observations of multicultural teams working together have, indeed, provided empirical evidence of a propensity for finding creative solutions to practical problems in such mixed settings.[5] This suggests a connection between multilingual workplace practices and economic processes in adding value. The potential for multicultural groups to be more productive is seen as linked to the fact that collectively, teams display broader knowledge of trends and issues and approach problems from different perspectives. In drawing on their various language repertoires, individual members activate diverse mental activities, thought patterns and knowledge systems as multiple keys to new concepts. In collaboration, this can generate a synergy of original ideas that manifests itself productively, enhancing team outcomes when faced with complex tasks.[6] An asset for organizations, this dynamic is found to release economic potential in providing creative approaches for product design, production processes and marketing strategies, and in forming new partnerships.

A drawback noted of multilingual group activity is that in tapping into multiple cultural perspectives, it may take team members longer to converge on an idea. Misunderstandings and uncertainty whether collaborating colleagues have made themselves clear to others may initially hamper progress. However, if managed appropriately, increased team creativity and member satisfaction can figure among the gains of multilingual collaboration.[7] Where innovation is valued over and above speed of production, a multilanguage workforce can be a creative solution to developing new, market-leading opportunities.

Nevertheless, a widespread strategy is to install a common language throughout the organization on the basis of the fact that it facilitates faster communication and helps shape the corporate image. Siemens is one of many international companies that uses English as the main language, despite its German roots. Often, English serves for specific functions and tasks within an organization such as in streamlining software systems, data storage and other forms of overarching corporate communications. For employees in such multinational settings, working in a lingua franca is the functional reality, with other languages used alongside.

Companies such as those featured above need to manage language use deliberately by equipping their employees to perform well in English and other strategic languages so as to operate in many markets worldwide.[8] But, as we saw earlier, language proficiency also needs to involve cultural awareness to build trust and prevent the risk of misunderstanding. This is essential in the case of international mergers such as Nissan-Renault, the Japanese–French alliance that has brought together workers from fundamentally divergent cultures.[9] Such companies benefit from recruiting bicultural individuals as go-betweens to prevent the emergence of possible cultural fault lines and conflicts in the workforce. One factor in the failed 1998 merger of Germany's Daimler Benz AG with the American Chrysler Corporation was the partners' cultural and linguistic incompatibility.[10] In another case, Swissair, the former 'Flying Bank', was likely affected by cultural challenges, which influenced the way decisions were made prior to its collapse in 2001.

Whether or not an international organization's policy is to use a single corporate language, research has shown that employees are prone to adopt a range of communication strategies in a variable, flexible and dynamic way. One mode chosen in multilingual interactions between partners from different language backgrounds is that everybody speaks in his or her own language and is expected to understand those used by the others. Known as receptive multilingual competence, this mode of communication is frequently seen to occur in quadrilingual Switzerland and also in Scandinavia, whose Germanic languages are largely mutually comprehensible and, hence, do not necessarily require interpreting. An example of this in fiction is the Nordic Noir hit 'The Bridge', where Saga Norén always talks in Swedish to her various Danish colleagues, who in turn reply in Danish. This type of multilingual practice is a cost-effective and democratic approach to communication management, and enables swift problem-solving, from production to sales.

Nevertheless, whichever corporate policy is ultimately relied upon, some translation is usually needed to facilitate multilingual communication, whether with colleagues from different overseas subsidiaries or for customer-facing roles. If such language-related tasks cannot be carried out in-house, they are, increasingly, outsourced to a language service provider.

Language services markets

The language services industry supplies a vast range of multilingual communication solutions at the interface of global markets. This type of business is booming, but it is not new. Already, millennia ago, paid language work was performed to facilitate cross-cultural communication for trade, as we saw with the bilingual interpreters used in King Hammurabi's Babylon. Now, an entire, largely Internet-driven, sector has evolved to deliver language support to enterprises and organizations intent on adapting their products and services for domestic and international customers. Among the fastest growing providers are firms that offer language and technological solutions with translation and interpreting as well as software engineering and website design. The modern language industry's market size is taking on global proportions, being forecast to rise in the United States to US\$ 47 billion by 2018.[11] This shows that outsourcing of language services is now a significant part of the global economy. It feeds on companies' rapid expansion overseas and is normal practice in many industries. In response, thousands of firms have mushroomed across the globe to meet the rising demand from multinational organizations for language work.

The major players in the field deliver specialized services for a diverse clientele. For example, Lionbridge covers website translation services, TransPerfect offers medical device solutions and Pearl Linguistics specializes in legal, banking and finance translations. Some providers work in a considerable range of languages, from Arabic to Pashto to Zulu, with translation services possible for rare combinations of the sets of languages covered. Others are branching out in anticipation of their public's complex needs for customized language solutions.[12] Smartling, a cloud-based translation firm, does just this, offering clients translations of their websites and apps into 'any language, all cultures, every market'.[13] To keep up with these developments, the industry needs language professionals who are acquainted with a combination of advanced software and specialist language skills. These employees are also expected to have in-depth knowledge of technical terminologies used for covering work commissioned by diverse clients, whether commercial litigation lawyers, engineering project managers or pharma security experts. Moreover, companies planning to export to other countries depend on the expertise of localization experts to ensure that the specifications of their products and services meet with the conventions and expectations in the targeted foreign markets. This also means adapting the tone, voice, concepts and images used in (online) advertising in a culturally appropriate and sensitive way without causing misunderstandings or offence among prospective consumers. Lessons have been learnt from misfired product launches as happened when the Scandinavian vacuum cleaner manufacturer Electrolux tried to advertise its goods in the United States with the ambiguous slogan 'Nothing sucks like an Electrolux'. Translators with various specializations are in demand everywhere and often work on projects from different agencies on a temporary, contract or freelance basis. They need to be able to proceed fast and accurately since often turnaround times are confirmed in advance to guarantee a prompt service. For example, Straker Translations claim on their website that they can offer a service that is '4x faster than industry average translation times'.[14]

Today, many service provider businesses work round the clock to connect diverse clients and communities. For example, having customized telephone sales and services that span continents in a range of target languages offers companies a competitive advantage. Every day, millions of consumer enquiries are answered, thousands of new websites are created and hundreds of books are translated, all in a myriad of languages. Often such work is outsourced to native speakers employed in foreign markets. A wave of relocated call centres overseas started in the early 2000s, most prominently with the Hong Kong and Shanghai Banking Corporation (HSBC) drawing on language service providers in India. Since then, armies of freelance workers have been hired from Manila to Bangalore and São Paulo by call centre agencies to supply otherwise well-resourced corporate clients relatively cheaply with the services they require. These employees often represent a link in a communication chain across time and space. For example, a Portuguese-speaking service can be delivered to clients around the world 24/7, through operators based, first, in Macau, then in Goa and, finally, in Cuba.

The massive movement of language services to delivery centres overseas has worked primarily because of its linkage of lower costs with availability of educated people willing to carry out routine work. But this highly fragmented industry relies on networks of firms subcontracting freelancers whose quality of service provision varies. With the gradually rising rates charged in the various service delivery regions, and possibly also as a result of cultural incompatibilities that can occur in such work, some companies (Santander, British Telecom and Aviva, to name but a few) have recently begun to relocate to language service centres closer to home.

The practice of outsourcing language work to service providers can, arguably, involve a range of risks, from financial to operational and managerial. Many of the industry's firms claim to be able to deliver translations of long texts into many languages quickly. This, combined with the competitively low rates charged for translation services, has unleashed a lively debate among service users and providers about quality guarantees. A new challenge has emerged with companies providing crowd-sourced translations. One such venture, OneHourTranslation,[15] promotes itself as a low-cost, fast service covering fourteen languages. The gamble made by prospective clients tempted with such offers is that they may end up with mistranslations carried out by people who are not qualified for this type of work. In some industries, for example the pharma sector, quality assurance is more critical than delivery speed or cost of a translation service. Pharmaceutical translations need to conform to the industry's compliance rules and guidelines. What is more, in the European Union, the different languages used on pharmaceutical labels must carry identical meanings. This means that translators are required to give more than just a literal translation of terms used in leaflets or on packaging.

The concern over confidentiality is another reason why some companies are reluctant to entrust their relationships to a third party. Any organization outsourcing to a third party is potentially vulnerable. Even where an agency guarantees security and confidentiality, there are occasions when the practice of outsourcing would be contrary to an organization's or the public's interests. This point was raised when the UK Ministry of Justice decided to outsource its multilingual needs to an external provider. Nevertheless, its court language services for foreign, deaf and hard-of-hearing defendants were privatized in 2012, which led to a number of counterproductive practices including ineffective or aborted trials that all had to be paid for at public expense.[16] Confidentiality is paramount where language services are required in the legal domain, for diplomacy, intelligence and security as well as in other public and private matters.

In response to an identified need of clients, an industry offshoot has been set up offering standards certification schemes for translation and related services. This move is backed by the Language Industry Associations in Europe, Canada and the United States[17] and other organizations that promote language services as a global business. With a view to capacity building, these professional bodies are also promoting work placement schemes as well as organizing internships for translation graduates new to the language services sector. Thus, in matching newly qualified people with companies and setting translation standards, these organizations are further consolidating the industry's position in the global marketplace.

In brief, the strong demand for professionals with multiple language capabilities to satisfy worldwide communication needs has engendered a booming trade. This market has many providers who compete as vendors of language products and services. In this line of business, language is used as a technical skill for the purpose of delivering information and for multilingual communication. Language occupies a central economic role in this services-based sector, whether as an outsourced activity or not. As new companies are trying to match demand with supply, they depend on a growing number of language specialists. In carrying out specific (translation, transcription or other) assignments, the industry's professionals are expected to aim for productivity, accuracy and efficiency in order to maintain customer satisfaction. As they are trained to perform language work, oral and written, their expertise becomes a resource with considerable revenue-generating potential. This means that the learning of languages as a core competence and essential skillset has growing economic relevance. Automated services such as Google Translate may in time displace some of this work, but they are not likely to replace it since cultural sensitivity, confidentiality and quality are central criteria in the language services sector. This market has corporate and individual customers and consumers of information buying language as a product, service or expertise. Language is a central resource for the distribution of many different services in the globalized economy. As a result, analysts[18] have identified the growing importance of language with exchange value in key economic areas including performance art, tourism and language teaching.

Language teaching industry

In today's world of service markets, where languages and bilingualism have come to be treated as economic commodities, approaches to language education are also changing. This can affect the choices made by institutions in allocating resources for language instruction and those made by people for learning particular languages (or not). Economically salient languages naturally enjoy a more viable position, which reflects their degree of use in transnational markets. The study abroad of various languages is often promoted by national institutions such as the Instituto Cervantes in Spain, the Alliance Française in France, the Goethe Institut in Germany, the Foundation for Japanese in Japan and the Confucius Institute in China. In addition to encouraging international cultural exchange and relations, these organizations also aim to extend the worldwide remit and use of their languages.

However, in today's knowledge economy, English clearly enjoys an (as yet) unrivalled advantage as a global language. The Teaching English as a Foreign Language (TEFL) industry invests enormous resources (through teachers, teaching materials and courses) in promoting it further on the international market. This has proved to be very successful. According to David Crystal, today two and a quarter billion people across the globe speak (some degree of) English, with roughly one billion actively studying it at any point in time in language schools from Azerbaijan to Vietnam.[19]

So for now, the TEFL industry is booming. It declares itself as providing the eighth largest source of earnings in the UK.[20] Its further, and rapid, expansion looks set as it supplies, and is simultaneously stimulated by, a huge global demand for its teaching. Its customers are no longer mainly from the business, scientific, legal, political and academic communities, but also include wide swathes of school populations, EU-wide and across the world, from Japan to India, Malaysia and Rwanda. To consolidate the market in this direction, new developments in English language teaching include culturally adapted online learning programmes and greater tailoring of general language courses for different learner needs and age groups. The British Council has produced a MOOC[21] as part of a drive to penetrate specific world regions, currently the Middle East and North Africa where English fluency is weak and unemployment rates high, especially among the younger generation. Claiming that employees with better English skills can on average enjoy salaries elevated by 5 per cent (in Tunisia) to as high as 200 per cent (in Iraq) in comparison to earnings of their counterparts with no English,[22] it aims to motivate a greater take-up of the language in these regions and to promote student mobility. This is already generating revenue, with a range of government-sponsored travel scholarships to study English abroad from source markets in China, Saudi Arabia, Kuwait and Brazil. In countries less able to support outbound student mobility (such as Oman, Algeria, Morocco and also Syria), the British Council acts as a key sponsor and provides services that include continuing professional development courses. Return gains that flow from these inputs come in the shape of different activities in an enlarged English speakers' market. The industry also benefits massively from supplying English language training at a stream of major international sports events, such as the Olympic Games hosted in China

(Summer 2008), Russia (Winter 2014) and Brazil (Summer 2016). With future contests in South Korea (Winter 2018) and Japan (Summer 2020), in addition to the next football World Cups in Russia (2018) and Qatar (2022), this trend will continue. The perhaps exotic location of many of these target countries is often used as a means of attracting people into the teaching market, with TEFL job offers from sites in Russia to Indonesia and China. There are numerous course providers, such as English First, China's largest English language training supplier, which proposes on its website that 'working with [us], you will be teaching the current and future leaders of China [and] be able to form your own opinion of this economic powerhouse'.[23]

Over the last few decades, the global economy has propelled English towards taking the lion's share of the language teaching industry. The underlying assumption is that a common language is an optimizing tool in the global market. Hence, demand for English, as the language of business and international commerce, is likely to remain strong. However, with the connectedness of international trade, people are always going to have to communicate with foreign producers, buyers and sellers. As noted before, the global market also depends on delivering goods and services to consumers who may not speak English. With new economies growing stronger in China, Latin America, India and more widely, other languages may come to be marketed and used more extensively. Among the prime candidates are Mandarin, Spanish, Hindi and Arabic, the world's most commonly spoken languages, besides English. This is likely, over time, to give way to a more diversified worldwide language teaching industry, with individuals needing to build more varied multilanguage competencies for access to international markets as well as to local ones affected by globalization. The future language dynamics in the global market could, in due course, well become a multilingual scenario alongside English.

Heritage and language tourism

It is relatively easy nowadays to get a close-up view of many 'indigenous' cultures. You can enjoy a meal in a Bedouin tent in the Arabian Desert, tour Pennsylvania in horse and buggy to learn about the Amish faith or 'chill out' with the Sami in Northern Scandinavia. Heritage marketing, a growing branch of the tourism industry, is in vogue. Numerous entrepreneurs around the world are setting up venues that offer a taste of 'the real thing'. Often, lesser-used languages are employed as a means to convey traditional culture that feeds the nostalgia of tourists, whether through ingredients listed in Basque on jam pots, creole gospel songs on a colonial trail in Haiti or guided tours in Welsh in the Patagonian Andes. Moreover, the use of community languages on heritage websites can serve as a commoditized resource more widely. Such place-marketing activities, whether real or staged, have proved their regenerative potential for economically peripheral regions by supplying local people with new employment opportunities to sell their products to tourists.

Maori in New Zealand, Welsh in the United Kingdom and Gaelic in parts of Ireland are among the many regional languages worldwide whose vitality has been boosted to some extent by their gaining economic value. Unlike other language-specific goods and services, this niche market does not depend on the demographic size of a language community. In fact, by exporting the idea of 'small is beautiful', it is likely to stimulate, and benefit from, the consumers' demand for something that is felt to be genuine and scarce. A branch of this sector caters for other kinds of clients wishing to reconnect with their ancestral language. In responding to their needs, the language heritage business has merged with education tourism as it offers a variety of short programmes, for example in Lithuanian or Yiddish at the historic University of Vilnius. In drawing on culture and language as a resource that is in demand, the remit of this sector is reaching way beyond its particular region.

Moreover, this language travel tourism is generating growing revenue for numerous international language education agencies promoting language study holidays abroad. This offers tailor-made packages with a wide range of exotic options that enable individuals to combine language study with their own interests. Tourists can get a flavour of variants of the Spanish language outside Europe on trips to Guatemala, Ecuador or Peru, brush up on their French skills alongside gastronomy courses in Monaco or learn elementary Chinese in a monastery as part of a hiking tour in Taipei's restricted mountain areas.[24] Some two million people take a trip abroad every year to learn a language for professional or personal purposes.[25] Added to this are school populations whom this market is targeting with proposals to 'discover a world beyond [the] classroom'[26] with educational trips to such antique sites as the excavated ruins of Pompeii in Italy, or to explore diverse mythological settings such as that of the Minotaur in Crete. Educational agents can respond to a variety of further offers for group excursions to selected sites such as Istanbul, Marrakech or Vietnam to experience different cultures and languages. This sector is consolidating its position in the market through standardized programme portfolios with mainstream solutions for group-based learning while also offering networked opportunities for language experiences through internships, volunteering opportunities or recreational activities in various host countries. Business performance in this trade is counted in turnover figures per student week on a course abroad. The revenue gained serves the overlapping interests of professionals, from language travel agencies to schools and national associations involved in language or educational travel.

The entire industry, with its various branches, illustrates perfectly how the importance of languages as a skill has increased over time. Languages have come to figure as commodities,[27] whether as conveyors of localization in niche markets or as technical skills in translation, as well as in merchandising their study abroad. As a tradable item, they have economic exchange value much like any other goods on the market. This multibillion dollar industry also promotes interest in a way of life, means of consumption and associated economies.

New languages, new markets

The dwarves invented a new language to trade with each other. There isn't any one 'dwarven' language.[28]

This extract from a discussion thread on the fantasy video game series 'Dragon Age' is about one of the story's tribes, the humanoid dwarves. Problems with infertility led to a decrease in their population and caused the loss of many of their languages. So they invented a 'common tongue' in order to trade with each other and later introduced this to other races. A whole roster of other made-up languages, whether Ander, Elvish or Tevene, is used in this virtual adventure world. Their fictional development reflects some of the themes touched on in this book. We have encountered a range of languages, some prospering as a vehicle of wider communication, others in decline. We have come across ad hoc jargons, pidgins and lingua francas used as a means to obtain commodities, information or resources for technological developments.

We have also looked into Esperanto that was intended as a neutral means of communication. Why has it not taken root more widely? According to the English philologist and writer J. R. R. Tolkien, constructed languages are dead if they are not steeped in legends.[29] He set out to create mythologies that resonate with the invented, variegated vocabularies of the language worlds in Middle Earth, from the delicate chimes of Elvish to the dark Black Speech of Sauron's sinister Mordor that puts a curse on anyone using it. The worldwide appeal of his epic fantasy novel 'The Lord of the Rings' drew attention to his languages. Its screenplay adaptation is counted among the highest grossing film franchises of all time, with additional revenue gained from follow-on home entertainment. Constructed languages also feature in many other fantasy creations that have become big business. In the realm of science fiction, aliens in *Avatar* speak Na'vi. Klingon, which features prominently in the *Star Trek* TV series and movies, has spawned a sizeable cultural following. The Klingon Language Institute provides language proficiency certification, and Klingonists can read publications in their adopted language including Khamlet by Wil'yam Shex'pir.[30]

A different series of (auxiliary) languages is instrumental in supporting this virtual world. Computer programmers use specially formulated codes such as Java, Python and C++ to drive the digital entertainment industry worldwide. Deploying structured commands, a growing generation of people engages asymmetrically with computers to create the architecture and extend the possibilities to enable media streaming, online gaming and social media interaction. The games sector enjoys an active market that is driven by faster and more powerful developments and the hunger of consumers for ever more immersive fantasy experiences. Many franchises have a core group of fans, generating a massive profit. Ranking highest in popularity currently is the video game series 'Call of Duty', which has sold over 175 million copies as of April 2015, securing US$10 billion in revenue.[31] By way of comparison, the annual sum of this income alone is roughly equivalent to the GDP of the Solomon Islands. The accumulated revenue gained from the full range of online games is of astronomical proportions, heralding a golden age of the virtual reality world. This success is due to the languages that computer programmers have invented for themselves. In turn, they will be able to harvest the fruits of the massively growing entertainment industry.

More fundamentally, the technology that programmers help generate drives the way we are engaging with the real world. In keeping up with the lifestyle many of us have come to expect today, we depend on experts with multiple coding skills to produce user-friendly platforms for real-time applications (as needed for mobile phones or cars), for crunching massive data sets (as in astrophysics or finance) and for virtual environments (as used for medical scanning, or for remote surgery). Psychologists employ multi-user systems in producing simulations, for example, to obtain a 3D representation of brain activity patterns when a multilingual individual engages in speech. A digital approach also serves as an educational tool for constructionist learning, that is, learning online by doing, and by building knowledge together. It can be used to galvanize creative approaches to problem-solving in virtual environments, and for experimental design or production solutions through participation of multilingual teams. In architecture, this could entail online collaboration on a housing regeneration project where innovative ideas are drawn from the participants' culturally diverging mindsets. Similarly LMOOCs, producing learning environments that combine education with social networking, can work to stimulate the students' progression. Linking up with entertainment, these massive online systems look set to transform the way many people learn.

Online educational entertainment enjoys a growing market as it connects language learning with hobbies, special interests and gaming. The industry's compelling audio-visual sceneries provide in-depth submersive experiences where languages are learnt interactively, while at the same time stimulating a learner's enjoyment and amusement. Such scenarios can be engrossing and educational if they are suited to the pace and interests of consumers. Without our visiting the country of the target language, virtual immersive environments enable us to retrace our own steps and learn a new language just as we did in childhood by listening, absorbing and speaking. An example is 'Little Pim', an entertainment method where young learners engage through live-action videos with the set's characters in another language. This package claims to make language learning easy by adjusting the speed and range of topics covered to the attention span of toddlers, even babies.[32]

It looks as if the central role that language plays in technology is ever diversifying. In many situations, we now require no human intermediary. With our devices, we can get almost instantaneous basic translations into an increasing range of languages from a visual, acoustic or written input. The clinician referred to in Chapter 3 who needed to understand quickly what her patient was saying could have done worse than resorting to Google Translate. Moreover, our relationship with smartphones has an effect on how we use languages and on how we learn and play. Intent on engaging in speedy and efficient exchanges, we rely on a profusion of acronyms and abbreviations such as lol ('laughing out loud') or g2g ('got to go'). In due course, the changing ways in which we communicate may even have an effect on how we think – and this will no doubt evolve in multiple ways, because we can now also use movement, voice, iris and fingerprint recognition to interact with interfaces as new ways of communicating. Just as different types of multifunctional click sounds are employed in the speech of the Xhosa, Jul'hoan or Taa populations in Southern Africa, so it may well be that the range of new gestures we are using with X-Box Kinect and Google Glass will in the future become part of our means of communicating. With the breakneck speed of digital developments, this could soon lead to more diverse goods and services that solve new problems, further enhance efficiency and are more convenient as we entertain and educate ourselves. Despite their costs, these technological advances are likely to benefit economic expansion. Thus, the cycle of language influencing economics and economies influencing language that we have seen throughout this book appears set to continue into the future.

AFTERWORD

With this book, you have crossed time and space witnessing how languages are used in the exchange of goods and knowledge between cultures. Along this journey, you have encountered travelling traders and raiders, colonizers and slaves, emperors and spies, miners and moguls. In their own ways, they all depended on understanding other people's languages. They proved inventive in their efforts to produce a good economic return across cultural divides. In the Old World, Babylonians used bilinguals as go-betweens for bartering with those from other places. Later, businessmen like Marco Polo learnt several languages, boosting trade as cross-cultural brokers. From the Middle Ages, tradesmen deployed their lingua franca for commercial pursuits in the Mediterranean. And in colonial times, indigenous populations invented ad hoc jargons for trade with Europeans. As imperial powers expanded their mercantile activities overseas, they exported their own languages, in time displacing others. English turned out to take the lead among the big contenders (French, Spanish, Portuguese, German and Russian) as the language of wider communication. Over time, their languages became symbols of national identity and unity.

There are numerous publications on the collective role of languages. This book is not one of them. Rather, like our distant traders, it deals with the practical use of languages in today's highly mobile societies. It looks at the impact of economic incentives that drive the language choices of governments, organizations and individuals in multilingual contexts. It outlines anticipated return on investments in languages, whether in terms of multilingualism-driven GDP growth, revenue gained through new markets or increased earnings. It then shifts the lens to the social dimension in decision-making about multilingualism. You have read how transportation fatalities, workplace accidents and medical delays can occur through miscommunication. You have seen how multilanguage skills are required in security services and the police to form a rapport with citizens. You have witnessed how economic growth affects small-language ecologies across the globe from the Andes to the Himalayas. By now you may have gained a clearer idea about the role of multilingualism in society and how it connects with economics.

Whether as a consumer, traveller or exporter, in public service or in policymaking, you will probably be familiar with challenges that can arise in multilingual communication. You may have reflected on how governments, organizations or individuals could respond to language diversity. You may like to take a more active part in debates about economic and social implications of multilingualism and want to weigh up its benefits and drawbacks. Or you might be wondering whether to invest time, effort and money in learning other languages yourself to access resources or for career purposes. Whatever the nature of your engagement with languages, my hope is that you will be able to draw on this book as a source of ideas about multilingualism and its social and market potential today.

NOTES

The list of websites referenced can also be found online at www.bloomsbury.com/Hogan-Brun-Linguanomics.

Setting the scene

1 'UK and US businesses losing out due to lack of language skills and cultural awareness in their workforces'. *IDMP Europe* (2015). This reports on a study of UK-based business leaders and US- based hiring managers, http://www.pmlive.com/pmhub/pharmaceutical_translation_services/conversis/press_releases/uk_and_us_businesses_losing_out_due_to_lack_of_language_skills_and_cultural_awareness_in_their_workforces.

2 This quote by Met commissioner Sir Bernard Hogan-Howe is in J. Davenort, 'Scotland Yard launches drive for bilingual recruits', *Evening Standard* (10 July 2015), http://www.standard.co.uk/news/london/scotland-yard-launches-drive-for-bilingual-recruits-10401809.html.

3 London Metropolitan Police recruitment drive (2016), http://www.metpolicecareers.co.uk/newconstable/.

4 (US) Military.com. Foreign Language Proficiency Pay/Foreign Language Proficiency Bonus, http://www.military.com/benefits/military-pay/special-pay/foreign-language-proficiency-and-proficiency-bonus.html.

5 Comment by National Security Education Programme Flagship student, http://www.nsep.gov/content/language-flagship.

6 Edwards (2013: 26).

7 '"English Only"' Rule at Lidl Shops Sparks Welsh Row', *BBC News Wales* (7 November 2014), http://www.bbc.co.uk/news/uk-wales-29956188.

8 'Welsh will "never be banned" from Stores, says Lidl', *BBC News Wales* (9 November 2014), http://www.bbc.co.uk/news/uk-wales-29976134.

Chapter 1

1 *Histories* (Book II, 86). Herodotus' description of the ancient traditions, politics and geography was originally in classical Greek (the accuracy of some details is occasionally disputed). This work is published in English as a collection called *The Histories* (see Bowden 1997). Reference here is made to Bowden's nine books (in Roman numerals) and paragraphs therein (in Arabic numerals): on the procedure of, and some of the beliefs surrounding, embalming bodies (II, 86); on the Phoenicians' extensive commerce with the Ancient Egyptians (III, 6); on the Phoenicians engaging in transit trade of goods in Egypt and Babylonia (I, 1); on imports from the Indian market (III, 107).

2 Mummies of either accidentally desiccated or deliberately preserved bodies have been found in different cultures on every continent. We know from excavated artefacts that mummification formed an integral part of Egyptian burial rituals from about 3400 BC. For information on the early use of amber in the Near East, see Gestoso, 'Amber in the Near East', *I-Mediat,* 2 (December 2008), http://www.academia.edu/241848/Amber_in_the_Ancient_Near_East.

3 *Histories* (Book II, 32). Nasamoneans are described as an Eastern Libyan tribe living near Mount Atlas.

4 On the role of non-verbal signals in social interactions, see Frith (2009).

5 *Histories* (IV, 196); on silent trade, see also Curtin (1984: 14f).

6 For more information on ancient trading practices, see Johnston (2006: 165f).

7 The quotes about the characteristics of the Central Asian steppe's nomads are from Golden (2011: 12, 15, 16); see ibid. for information on multilingualism on the Silk Road (p. 24f) and for details about Sogdian traders (p. 50).

8 For more information on early trading communities, diaspora and routes, see Curtin (1984).

9 Hammurabi, king of the thriving city-state of Babylon (1792–1750 BC), extended his rule throughout Mesopotamia.

10 For information on bilingualism in ancient societies, see Adams, Janse and Swain (2002).

11 The Rosetta Stone, carved in 196 BC, contains an ancient royal decree with writing on it in two languages (Egyptian and Greek), in the three scripts (hieroglyphic, demotic and Greek) being used in Egypt at the time.

12 Darius the Great was king of the Persian Empire between 522 BC till his death in 486 BC.

13 The Behistun Inscription – actually three large separate texts inscribed in stone on different parts of a mountainside – is said to be to cuneiform writing what the Rosetta Stone is to hieroglyphs.

14 Pliny the Elder, *Natural History*, VII, 24 (see English translation by Bostock and Riley 1855).

15 Mahaffy (2014: 466).

16 For information on ancient empires, communication and the development of writing systems, see Innis (1950).

17 On the history and introduction of Hindu-Arabic Numerals, see Smith and Karpinski (1911).

18 The descendants of Latin (nowadays classified as Romance languages) include Italian, French, Spanish, Portuguese, Romanian, Catalan, Provençal and Romansh (a language spoken in parts of Switzerland).

19 Procopius' description of how Emperor Justinian acquired knowledge about silk worms (originally in *History of the Wars*, 8.17.1-7) is in Page, Capps and Rouse (1928: 229–30).

20 This period of protection became known as Pax Sinica (Latin for Chinese peace), similar in aim to the Pax Mongolica and the Pax Romana.

21 On the practice of interpreting in early imperial China, see Lung (2011: 61–2).

22 The quote of the letter by Pope Innocent IV to Khan Güyük is in De Rachewiltz (1972: 87). Further information on the Mongolians is in Golden (2011: 76–90).

23　This quote from Marco Polo is in Latham (1958: 8). The
    original travelogue entitled *Il Milione* was written in 1298
    by the Old French writer Rustichello from stories narrated
    by Marco Polo while both were in prison in Genova. The
    correctness of this account (which was published during his
    lifetime) has been queried, but it is found to be mostly accurate
    as regards its cultural information. The Polos were not the first
    Westerners who had reached China.

24　Latham (1958: 57).

25　Ibid.: 211.

26　Ibid.: 148.

27　Ibid.: 211.

28　Ibid.: 118.

29　The information on the spread of the Black Death comes
    from *Channel 4* (2008), http://www.channel4.com/history/
    microsites/H/history/a-b/blackdeath.html.

30　For more details on Gabriele de' Mussi's account of the plague
    in Kaffa (originally entitled *Istoria de morbo sive mortalitate
    que fuit de 1348*), see Deaux (1969: 43–4). On the idea that
    what happened in Kaffa was an act of biological warfare, see
    Wheelis (2002).

31　For a discussion of household inventory studies from the
    Netherlands and England showing the demand for imported
    goods in Western Europe in the closing decades of the
    seventeenth century, see McCants (2007).

32　Pinker (1994: 33). Various pidgin languages have been used
    in many locations and times for trade purposes. They can be
    based on any language (e.g. Nigerian pidgin or the Cameroon
    pidgin are based on English). The term pidgin is possibly
    derived from the Chinese pronunciation of the word 'business',
    used when the English established their first Chinese trading
    post (in 1664 at Canton). On trade languages, see also Edwards
    (2012: 47–52).

33　For further information, see Siegel (2008).

34　On linguistic imperialism, see Phillipson (2009). He sees the
    internationalization process and the relationship between
    powerful and lesser-used languages as symbolic power in

action, and linguistic capital, its acquisition and investment, as a prime example of symbolic power in use, with key examples in commerce, science and publication.

35 A movable type system for printing made of ceramic materials was already in use earlier in ancient China and also in Korea. Around 1450, Gutenberg developed this further using the alphabet, which was quicker.

36 For critical reflections between languages, nations and printers, see Anderson (1991). He sees printers as early examples of modern capitalism and links printing languages with their role as collective identity markers during phases of nation building.

37 Rare earth metals are commonly defined as the seventeen elements in the periodic table made up of the fifteen lanthanides plus scandium and yttrium. China has held a near monopoly in this market for well over a decade as the main supplier to meet the global demand for rare earth metals. Attracted by lower taxes and cheap labour, many Western hi-tech companies (Apple and Nokia, to name but two) set up their manufacturing plants in China.

38 For information on Mandarin Chinese taught in UK schools, see British Association for Chinese Studies (BACS), http://bacsuk. org.uk/chinese-in-uk-schools.

Chapter 2

1 The 1977 *Charter of the French Language* (Loi 101) made French the official language in Quebec. A subsequent modification (Loi 104) requires that French be predominant on commercial signs. The language watchdog 'Office de la langue française' oversees language practices in the public domain and has powers to take appropriate measures to promote the use of French.

2 *CBC News Montreal* (12 June 2015), http://www.cbc.ca/news/ canada/montreal/quebec-to-tighten-language-law-force-retailers-to-add-french-descriptions-to-names-1.3111750.

3 The regulations on language practice for business in Quebec are drawn from Lizotte (2014), https://www.osler.com/uploadedFiles/News_and_Resources/Publications/Guides/Doing_Business_in_Canada_-_2011/DBIC-Chapter17.pdf.

4 These 1980s figures are taken from Coulmas (1992: 94).

5 Ridler and Pons-Ridler (1986).

6 For a summary analysis, see Vaillancourt (1996).

7 Bourhis (1984). Comments on the current situation in Quebec are by Tourigny (personal communication).

8 For a review of findings on language and the socio-economic status in Quebec, see Vaillancourt (1996).

9 These results are presented in Grin (2003).

10 Saiz and Zoido (2005).

11 These findings are presented in Grin, Sfreddo and Vaillancourt (2010).

12 Bleakley and Chin (2004).

13 Chiswick and Miller (2007).

14 This quote is often attributed to the sociologist W. B. Cameron.

15 See Grin and Vaillancourt (1997).

16 An economically propelled example is the change to bilingualism from French in German Saarland (see Chapter 3).

17 Grin, Sfreddo and Vaillancourt (2009).

18 Ibid.

19 'The Impact of Foreign Languages on British Business'. Language Survey, British Chambers of Commerce (2004).

20 'Effects on the European Economy of Shortages of Foreign Language Skills in Enterprise' (ELAN). The National Centre for Languages (December 2006), http://ec.europa.eu/languages/policy/strategic-framework/documents/elan_en.pdf.

21 Gazzola and Grin (2013).

22 EurActiv (2006). The European Union's estimated annual expenditure on translation costs is €330 million (European Commission. Translation, 2016), http://www.euractiv.com/culture/parliament-cuts-translation-budg-news-516201.

23 The Economist Intelligence Unit Report (2012), http://www. economistinsights.com/sites/default/files/legacy/mgthink/ downloads/Competing%20across%20borders.pdf; more details on this are in Chapter 3.

24 The policy also provoked concern among the minority Anglophone speakers in Quebec. Many responded by emigrating to other parts of Canada. Even today, Quebec has a negative net internal migration rate, although its overall population is increasing as a result of positive net international migration.

25 Kelly, DePalma and Stewart (2009).

26 Morelle (3 September 2014), http://www.bbc.co.uk/news/ science-environment-29037168. See also Worstall (9 March 2014), http://www.forbes.com/sites/timworstall/2014/09/03/ language-extinction-is-driven-by-economic-growth-and-success/#7fa33a42a551.

27 Amano et al. (2014). This group of researchers (from the Universities of Cambridge, Oxford, Cornell, Copenhagen and Palaiseau) examined environmental and social economic drivers affecting language decline. Using species diversity as a basis for language diversity, they worked out that 25 per cent of languages (1,705 out of a total of 6,909) around the world are under threat. They calculated the extinction risk for languages using three criteria: (1) a small geographic range of speakers (291 languages are spoken in areas of less than 20 km^2); (2) a small population size (there are 1,496 languages with less than 1,000 speakers each); (3) a rapid decline in speaker numbers (168 languages have suffered a decline of more than 30 per cent over three generations).

28 May (2001).

29 Flores Rivera has over 1.3 million views on YouTube, https://www.youtube.com/watch?v=BvT9y0HqItE. On the (underlying) issue touched on here of linguistic justice and considerations of fairness for language policy decisions, see the International Association of Language Commissioners, http:// languagecommissioners.org/welcome.php.

30 The UK government is one of twenty-five states that have ratified the European Charter for Regional or Minority

Languages (ECRML), http://conventions.coe.int/Treaty/EN/Treaties/Html/148.htm. Without being legally binding, this treaty aims to protect and promote regional and minority languages as a threatened aspect of Europe's cultural heritage. The Scots Gaelic language development body *Bòrd na Gàidhlig* was established in 2005 with a view to securing the status of the Gaelic language as an official language of Scotland.

31 World Language Advancement Act (16 July 2015), http://www.languagepolicy.org/news/members-of-congress-introduce-world-language-advancement-act/.

32 Crystal, The History of English, *BBC Voices* (November 2004), http://www.davidcrystal.com/?fileid=-4051.

33 Blommaert (2010).

34 '270 Nationalities and 300 Different Languages: How a United Nations of Workers is Driving London Forward', *Evening Standard News* (1 March 2011), http://www.standard.co.uk/news/270-nationalities-and-300-different-languages-how-a-united-nations-of-workers-is-driving-london-6572417.html.

Chapter 3

1 This quote comes from Baron (2004).

2 Loss aversion, where monetary losses (through expenditure) can loom larger than actual gains in decision-making, has been identified as a characteristic in behavioural economics; see Levitt and List (2008).

3 Details on this and other fateful air crashes caused by misunderstandings, and the additional data from the NASA study are in Baron (2004).

4 The Korean Air story is in Gladwell (2009).

5 See online information supplied by Airbus on new voice-recognition technology, http://www.airbus.com/newsevents/news-events-single/detail/speaking-the-right-language-airbus-explores-innovative-voice-recognition-technology-for-the-air-tra/.

6   More information on language and cultural diversity affecting safety in shipping, including data on the composition of multinational crew members, is in Hetherington, Flin and Mearns (2006).

7   Examples of maritime accidents through miscommunication among multinational crew members can be found in Grech, Horberry and Koester (2008).

8   This and other examples of maritime accidents through problems with multilingual communication are referred to in the *MARCOM Project* (see European Union-DG VII 1999).

9   Personal communication (August 2014). Further information on multilingual communication needs in healthcare settings comes from personal research for the EUROCITIES WG Health and Well-being.

10 For more information, see Società Italiana Telemedicina, http://www.sanitaelettronica.it.

11 According to a personal communication (May 2014), when dedicated dual telephone handsets are not available, a single receiver is passed back and forth, which works in a clinic setting but is more difficult if the patient is in bed.

12 Anonymous communication by a clinician (6 December 2015).

13 The language-related workplace safety data across different sectors referred to here are reported in Lindhout et al. (2012: 137–69).

14 The Seveso Directive on prevention, preparedness and response, http://ec.europa.eu/environment/seveso/.

15 Stephenson (2015), http://www.bbc.co.uk/news/magazine-33019838.

16 Tutt et al. (2011: 5).

17 The Dutch language barrier project to improve workplace safety and efficiency is discussed in Paul (2013: 65–72); see also GlobalWorkTalk, http://www.global-work-talk.eu, which gives tips on work safety in multilingual workplaces.

18 For more details of multilingual policies and practices in an urban environment, see Matras and Robertson (2015: 310).

19 Cable Car of Mount Titlis with sign in Hindi, https://anilcm.wordpress.com/2015/03/15/wpc-sign/.

20 Migrants-to-Migrants (Mi-Mi), http://citiesofmigration.ca/wp-content/uploads/about-mimi-programme.pdf.

21 Welcoming Migrants and Refugees Forum, http://migrantforum.org.uk.

22 For more details, see: Blackledge and Creese (2010).

23 The EUROCITIES Integrating Cities Charter aims to harness the duties and responsibilities of European cities to promote equal opportunities for all residents, to integrate migrants and to embrace the diversity of their populations, http://www.integratingcities.eu/integrating-cities/integrating_cities_charter.

24 This project, supported by Creative Europe, promotes the idea of cultural and creative industries contributing to social innovation, inclusion and intercultural dialogue, http://www.cultureforcitiesandregions.eu.

25 This extract comes from Genesis (11.1-9) of the Bible's Old Testament.

26 Coulmas (1992: 90).

27 Lindhout et al. (2012: 139).

28 Pinker (1994: 16).

29 Frustrated by the political quarrels of his time, Ludwik Lejzer Zamenhof (a physician and writer of Jewish Polish descent) developed Esperanto in 1873 as a universal communication tool.

30 On the move to promote Esperanto for business, see: *The New York Times* (16 February 1921), http://query.nytimes.com/gst/abstract.html?res=9802E6D9123CE533A25755C1A9649C946095D6CF.

31 According to the Central Intelligence Agency (CIA) *World Fact Book,* https://www.cia.gov/library/publications/the-world-factbook/, only some 5.6 per cent of the world's total population speaks English as a primary language. That number doubles when people who speak English as a second or third language are counted. See also endnote 19 in Chapter 5.

32 See *Mercator Newsletter*, 98 (January 2014), http://www.mercator-research.eu/news/newsletter/.

33 Human capital is more widely defined as the stock of knowledge, habits, social and personality attributes, including

language and creativity as embodied in the ability to perform labour. This may be a collection of individual or social resources that can produce economic value.

34 For information on foreign language learning at primary and secondary schools in EU member states, see *Eurostat. Foreign Language Learning Statistics* (January 2016), http://ec.europa.eu/eurostat/statistics-explained/index.php/Foreign_language_learning_statistics.

35 Skorton and Altschuler, *FORBES. Education* (27 August 2012), http://www.forbes.com/sites/collegeprose/2012/08/27/americas-foreign-language-deficit/#1250035382f1.

36 The European Union's 1+2 language learning model proposes that all children learn two languages, in addition to their own; see *Common European Framework of Reference for Languages: Learning, Teaching, Assessment* (CEFR), http://www.coe.int/t/dg4/linguistic/Source/Framework_EN.pdf.

37 If successful, this legislation would reinstate a grant competition in the Department of Education for state and local education agencies to establish, improve or expand language instruction programmes, see www.languagepolicy.org.

38 Nevadomski Berdan, 'Computer Science Is Not a Foreign Language', *Huffington Post. Education* (22 April 2014), http://www.huffingtonpost.com/stacie-nevadomski-berdan/computer-science-is-not-a_b_4823691.html.

39 See also the article Johnson, 'Why Language Isn't Computer Code', *The Economist, Language and Computers* (31 July 2012) and the comment (cstaley, 31 July 2012) that human language is a more sophisticated medium than code, http://www.economist.com/blogs/johnson/2012/07/language-and-computers.

40 The chief proponent of a community-based multicultural language policy for Australia was Lo Bianco (1987).

41 Macgibbon, 'A Nation Lost in Translation', *The Sydney Morning Herald. National* (7 February 2011), http://www.smh.com.au/national/education/a-nation-lost-in-translation-20110206-1aifl.html#ixzz3pnlnNSjK.

42 Extra and Yağmur (2012).

43 Cummins and Swain (1986).

44 On the European Union's understanding of language competencies as a composite resource, see Multilingualism and the Common European Framework, http://www.languageportfolio.ch/page/content/index.asp?MenuID=2496&ID=4189&Menu=17&Item=6.2.4.

45 University of Cambridge, http://www.becambridge.com/applying/choosing-a-course/modern-and-medieval-languages-mml/.

46 Yale University. Near Eastern Languages and Civilizations, http://nelc.yale.edu.

47 Global 30. 'Global 30 to invite 300,000 international students to Japan', http://www.uni.international.mext.go.jp/global30/.

48 Skolkovo Institute of Science and Technology, http://www.skoltech.ru/en/admissions/.

49 'More English Instruction Slated For France', *ICEF Monitor* (2013), http://monitor.icef.com/2013/06/more-english-instruction-slated-for-france/.

50 Budapest University of Technology and Economics. Office of International Education, https://kth.bme.hu/en/oie.

51 Zürich Hochschule für Angewandte Wissenschaften (ZHAW), http://gaia.zhaw.ch/alfresco/guestDownload/direct?path=/webdav/Publikationen/Modulbeschreibungen/ModuleDescription_w.BA.XX.1SuR2-BL.XX.pdf.

52 Free University of Bolzano/Bozen, http://www.mastersportal.eu/universities/860/free-university-of-bozen-bolzano.html.

53 Australian National University. International Security Studies, http://asiapacific.anu.edu.au/students/undergrad/international-security.

54 National Security Language Initiative for Youth (NSLI-Y), http://exchanges.state.gov/us/program/national-security-language-initiative-youth-nsli-y.

The need for language skills for national security had been established previously at the level of Congress in the United States. In 1957, after the Russians launched Sputnik, President Eisenhower committed federal support funds for foreign language instruction as part of the National Defence Education Act (see also reference in endnote above).

55 See (US) Military Rates. Inventive and Special Pay, http://www.
militaryrates.com/military-pay-incentives. The 'critical need'
languages are listed on page xi.

56 The British Army. Education on Operations, http://www.army.
mod.uk/training_education/25235.aspx.

57 *Languages: The State of the Nation.* British Academy
Report (2003), http://www.britac.ac.uk/policy/state_of_the_
nation_2013.cfm.

58 These figures are taken from 'The Future of Universities. The
Digital Degree', *The Economist* (28 June 2014), http://www.
economist.com/news/briefing/21605899-staid-higher-education-
business-about-experience-welcome-earthquake-digital.

59 'Global Review Maps the State of MOOCs in 2014', *ICEF
Monitor* (2014), http://monitor.icef.com/2015/01/global-review-
maps-state-moocs-2014/.

60 'Travailler en français', https://sites.google.com/site/
mooctravaillerenfrancais/home.

61 'FutureLearn. Innovation: Key to Business Success', https://
www.futurelearn.com/courses/innovation-the-key-to-business-
success.

62 'Sarah Palin says Immigrants to the US Should "Speak
American"', *The Guardian*, Reuters (7 September 2015), http://
www.theguardian.com/us-news/2015/sep/07/sarah-palin-says-
immigrants-to-the-us-should-speak-american. Plus online
comments.

63 For information on portfolio-based language assessment as
a standard feature of language instruction for immigrants to
Canada, see: Immigration.ca. Live and work in Canada, http://
immigration.ca/en/.

64 On language requirements for adult migrants in Council of
Europe member states, see Extramiana and Van Avermaet
(2011). Scales of language proficiency levels range from basic
to advanced (or from A1–C2, according to the Common
European Framework of Reference; for more information, see
endnote 38 in Chapter 4).

65 For an assessment of discourses on national language testing
procedures for migrants across Europe, see Hogan-Brun,

Mar-Molinero and Stevenson (2009). On challenges of assessing language proficiency in the context of migration, consult the Association of Language Testers in Europe (ALTE), http://www.alte.org, who work towards ensuring fairness in testing.

66 Denmark's CPR (Det Centrale Personenregister) number can be obtained at the civil registration office (Folkeregistrieret) upon presentation of a residence permit, an ID and a passport. It is offered to anyone who can show that they have established a genuine and effective residence (job or sufficient funding) and address.

67 Asthana, *The Guardian* (29 March 2016), http://www.theguardian.com/politics/2016/mar/28/vote-leave-releases-list-of-serious-crimes-by-eu-citizens-in-britain.

Chapter 4

1 Doug Ahmann's comment is quoted and discussed in the Freakonomics.com webpage by Lechtenberg, in 'Is Learning a Foreign Language Really Worth it? A New Freakonomics Radio Podcast' (6 March 2014), http://freakonomics.com/podcast/is-learning-a-foreign-language-really-worth-it-a-new-freakonomics-radio-podcast/.

2 Johnson, 'What Is a Foreign Language Worth?', *The Economist* (11 March 2014), http://www.economist.com/blogs/prospero/2014/03/language-study.

3 US population estimates (2015), https://www.census.gov/popest/data/national/totals/2014/index.html.

4 Moore, 'How Good Really Is Mark Zuckerberg's Mandarin?', *The Telegraph* (24 October 2014), http://www.telegraph.co.uk/technology/mark-zuckerberg/11182575/How-good-really-is-Mark-Zuckerbergs-Mandarin.html.

5 Guo, *The New York Times* (26 October 2015), http://www.nytimes.com/2015/10/27/technology/facebook-zuckerberg-china-speech-tsinghua.html.

6 The data of the reported survey are drawn from in-depth interviews carried out cross-globally in 2012 with 572 executives.

7   *Economist Intelligence Unit report* (2012: 9), http://www. economistinsights.com/sites/default/files/legacy/mgthink/ downloads/Competing%20across%20borders.pdf.

8   Dacey, *Swiss News SWI* (20 October 2010), http://www. swissinfo.ch/eng/bankrolling-a-new-swiss-resort/28577428.

9   Hardie is quoted in Reisz, 'Language Degrees: When the words are not enough', *Times Higher Education* (11 December 2014: 12).

10   Lightfoot, 'MBAs Need to Teach Soft Skills', *The Guardian* (9 December 2014: 4). The source given for the ten soft skills is Hult Labs. The other listed skills are self-awareness, integrity, team skills, critical thinking, comfort with ambiguity and uncertainty, creativity, execution and sales.

11   Quoted in *The Guardian* (2014); see endnote above.

12   Neeley and Kaplan, 'What's Your Language Strategy?', *Harvard Business Review* (September 2014), https://hbr.org/2014/09/ whats-your-language-strategy.

13   The reported findings of the 2013 British Council Report on 'Culture at Work' are based on a survey of HR managers at 367 large employers in nine countries: Brazil, China, India, Indonesia, Jordan, South Africa, the United Arab Emirates, the United Kingdom and the United States, https://www. britishcouncil.org/organisation/policy-insight-research/research/ culture-work-intercultural-skills-workplace.

14   Kate's comment (12 March 2014) is in reply to the article on the Freakconomics.com webpage by Lechtenberg (see endnote 1 above), http://freakonomics.com/podcast/is-learning-a-foreign-language-really-worth-it-a-new-freakonomics-radio-podcast/?c_ page=2#comments_archived.

15   Erard (2011).

16   Hunter, *Journal* (20 January 1788: 60–1), http://www.sl.nsw. gov.au/discover_collections/history_nation/terra_australis/ journals/hunter/index.html.

17   Google, https://translate.google.co.uk/about/intl/en_ALL/ languages.html. Microsoft Skype translator, https://support. skype.com/en/faq/FA34543/what-languages-are-available-in-skype-translator.

18 This communication comes from Brown (1 February 2016).

19 For more detailed information on the estimated numbers of speakers of English, see endnote 19 in Chapter 5. The other data in this paragraph are taken from the World Languages section of Ethnologue, http://www.ethnologue.com/statistics/size.

20 Bhattacharjee, 'Why Bilinguals are Smarter', *The New York Times* (Sunday Review) (17 March 2012), http://www.nytimes.com/2012/03/18/opinion/sunday/the-benefits-of-bilingualism.html?_r=0.

21 Georgetown University Medical Center, 'Bilinguals of Two Spoken Languages Have More Grey Matter Than Monolinguals', *Science Daily* (16 July 2015), www.sciencedaily.com/releases/2015/07/150716135054.htm.

22 Iha, *The Guardian* (18 February 2011), http://www.theguardian.com/science/2011/feb/18/bilingual-alzheimers-brain-power-multitasking.

23 Keim, *Science. Wired* (24 April 2012), http://www.wired.com/2012/04/language-and-bias/.

24 On cognitive benefits of bilingualism, see Cummins and Swain (1986); see also Mackey, 'The Case for Language Learning. What Happens In the Brain When You Learn a Language?' *Guardian Online* (4 September 2014), http://www.theguardian.com/education/2014/sep/04/what-happens-to-the-brain-language-learning.

25 'The Many Ways In Which Languages Boost Brain Power'. Association for Language Learning, http://www.all-languages.org.uk/news/features/speaking_your_mind_links_between_languages_and_other_skills.

26 See research by Keysar, Hayakawa and An, *Psychological Science*, 23/6 (2012: 661–8).

27 Fabrici (1601: 64), https://books.google.co.uk/books?id=nir o7RPZr7UC&pg=PA59&lpg=PA59&dq=Fabrici,+G.+(160 1),+De+Locutione&source=bl&ots=FElZPmobxG&sig=v7Z eWb_WvU0WVuMBnuvs_Lf_iS4&hl=en&sa=X&ved=0ah UKEwiW6pi2huvKAhXFChoKHTE2AaoQ6AEIPjAF#v=on epage&q=Fabrici%2C%20G.%20(1601)%2C%20De%20 Locutione&f=false. Charles V (1500–58) is thought to have had two native tongue(s) (French and Dutch), having grown up in

Ghent and Paris. The politics of the Holy Roman Empire are known to have involved an ongoing political conflict between the different feudal states of Germany.

28 On emotions and multilingualism, see Pavlenko (2006).

29 Languages for the Future (2013). British Council, https://www. britishcouncil.org/organisation/policy-insight-research/research/ languages-future. The other listed languages are Dutch, Polish, Hindi, Korean, Farsi, Swedish and Indonesian.

30 The public announcement, made by Baroness Coussins, Chair of the All Party Parliamentary Group on Modern Languages (APPG), is quoted in Richardson, *BBC News* (14 July 2014), http://www.bbc.co.uk/news/education-28269496.

31 These are France, Germany, Italy, the United Kingdom, Japan, the United States, Canada and Russia. They hold an annual meeting to foster consensus on global issues such as economic growth and crisis management, global security, energy and terrorism.

32 European Commission. Translation, http://ec.europa.eu/dgs/ translation/translating/officiallanguages/index_en.htm.

33 Lewis (2014).

34 Duolingo (twenty-five languages, currently ranging from Danish to Esperanto, Klingon and Swahili), https://www.duolingo. com. Among other online programmes are Lingvist (currently covering eight languages), https://www.lingvist.io; Memrise (over two hundred languages), https://www.memrise.com.

35 Hickey (2015: 28).

36 This quote is in Hickey (above). In the case of Duolingo, the drop-off rate is some seventy million, leaving some fifteen million active; see previous endnote. Other online language learning resources currently available are Vistawide (vistawide.com), which provides a host of links on ways of engaging with languages, through press displays, live broadcasts, foreign language film and music sites, bulletin boards and chat rooms in various languages, as well as offering career and study abroad advice, plus job listings for different languages. EUROLINGUA (http://www.eurolingua. com) and Voxy have a platform for personalized language support. Italiki (http://www.italki.com) is an online site that

connects learners with native speakers for personal language lessons. <TuneIn> is an online repository of radio stations from around the world.

37 An example of an online language community is Mylanguage Exchange (http://mylanguageexchange.com), which currently connects language exchange partners in over 133 countries, practising some 115 languages. Many other free online services and search databases (e.g. eTandem or Polyglot) exist that help connect speaking partners as per their language needs, age and interests, and for nearly every language, even those that are less commonly taught.

38 The CEFR assessment grid is available at Europass, https://europass.cedefop.europa.eu/en/resources/european-language-levels-cefr.

39 'Germany: B2 general + C1 medical = the new language skill code for foreign doctors'. *We Care that You Care* (2014), http://www.bleedle.net/germany-b2-general-c1-medical-the-new-language-skill-code-for-foreign-doctors/.

40 See also Chapter 3, under Harnessing Mobile Resources.

41 Target Jobs. Finance (8 December 2015), https://targetjobs.co.uk/career-sectors/investment-banking-and-investment/418374-speaking-another-language-can-help-you-get-a-graduate-investment.

42 See previous endnote.

43 Neeley and Kaplan (2014), https://hbr.org/2014/09/whats-your-language-strategy.

44 Davies, 'Demand for Speakers of Native Languages Fuels Pick-up in Hiring', *Financial Times. Working in International Banking* (24 April 2014), http://www.ft.com/cms/s/2/27ddcfbe-c3be-11e3-a8e0-00144feabdc0.html#axzz3tedRkOiv.

45 Lane, 'Language Skills Add to Job Prospects', *The Australian Higher Education* (27 December 2013), http://www.theaustralian.com.au/higher-education/language-skills-add-to-job-prospects/story-e6frgcjx-1226790285277.

46 The eleven official languages in Canada's Northwest Territories (which is more than in any other political division in the

Americas) are Chipewyan, Cree, English, French, Gwich'in, Inuinnaqtun, Inuktitut, Inuvialuktun, North Slavey, South Slavey and Tlinchon. Bilingual positions for public service in NWT are advertised on: Northwest Territories. Human Resources. 1208 Bilingual Bonus, http://www.hr.gov.nt.ca/human-resource-manual/1200-allowances-and-benefits/1208-bilingual-bonus.

47 Translation in the European Union – Facts and Figures, http://one-europe.info/translation-in-the-european-union-facts-and-figures.

48 Remark! is an example of a Deaf-led organization offering translation, interpretation and training services, http://www.remark.uk.com.

49 Galilea3 – The multilingual marketplace for freelancers, http://erlibird.com/go/galilea3.

Chapter 5

1 IBM Workforce Diversity, https://www.google.co.uk/search?client=safari&rls=en&q=07.ibm.com/ibm/au/corporateresponsibility/pdfs/GL_9833_diversity_nocov.08.pdf&ie=UTF-8&oe=UTF-8&gfe_rd=cr&ei=X9O9VoPRM6mx8wew5qS4Dg.

2 Airbus. People and Culture, http://www.airbus.com/company/people-culture/.

3 For more information, see endnote 6 in Chapter 4.

4 Michelin. Innovation for Improved Mobility, http://jobs.michelinman.com/eng/get-to-know-us/discover-michelin#c-diversity.

5 These surveys on multilingual workplace practices and communication strategies were carried out as part of an EU-funded programme on 'Language Dynamics and Management of Diversity' (DYLAN 2006–11), http://www.dylan-project.org/Dylan_en/index.php.

6 On the economic potential of multilingual co-construction and creative solutions for complex tasks, see Grin, Sfreddo and Vaillancourt (2010).

7   On the cost-effectiveness of multilingual solutions in companies including the use of receptive multilingual competence, see Berthoud, Grin and Lüdi (2013); see also Angouri and Strubell (2013).

8   Neeley and Kaplan (September 2014), https://hbr.org/2014/09/whats-your-language-strategy.

9   The reality for businesses is that different cultures exhibit various attitudes towards hierarchy or uncertainty, achievement and loyalty. Western societies (e.g. Americans or Canadians) are regarded as 'low-context' cultures that are more literal, analytic and action-oriented. Conversely, high-context cultures (the Chinese, Mexicans or Japanese) are seen to be more contemplative and time-rich, with greater attention paid to gestures and the overall tone of an interaction; see Solomon (2011).

10 The Economist Intelligence Report (2012: 10), http://www.economistinsights.com/sites/default/files/legacy/mgthink/downloads/Competing%20across%20borders.pdf.

11 Statista. The Statistics Portal. Language Services Industry In the US, http://www.statista.com/statistics/257656/size-of-the-global-language-services-market/.

12 On the developments in the language services market, see DePalma et al. (2014).

13 Smartling, https://www.smartling.com/?creative=79922596626&keyword=smartling&matchtype=e&network=g&device=c&gclid=CKXiwY6b_8gCFaoEwwodIuQECQ.

14 Straker Translations, https://www.strakertranslations.co.uk/?ag=5494114781&gclid=CJKipM6jiMkCFUEaGwodrLgKxA.

15 OneHourTranslation, https://www.onehourtranslation.com.

16 Maniar, 'Shambolic and Unworkable: Outsourcing of Court Interpreting Services', *Institute of Race Relations* (14 February 2013), http://www.irr.org.uk/news/shambolic-and-unworkable-outsourcing-of-court-interpreting-services/.

17 Quality standards for translation include EN 15038 in Europe, the CAN CGSB 131.10 in Canada and ASTM F2575-06 in the United States.

18 Among language analysts who comment on the growing importance of language as a resource with exchange value

(meaning that it can be monetized) in the globalized economy and on the role of languages in commodification processes are Heller (2010); Uricuoli and LaDousa (2013).

19 Crystal (2003) estimates that between 320 and 380 million speakers have English as their primary language (in Australia, Canada, New Zealand, the United Kingdom and the United States, often also described as the 'inner circle'); between three hundred and five hundred million people use it as their second tongue in countries where it may serve in the public sector and often for national commerce (in India, Nigeria, Bangladesh, Pakistan, Malaysia, Tanzania, Kenya, described as the 'outer circle'); between five hundred million and one billion use it widely for international communication (as in China, Indonesia, Russia or Brazil – the 'expanding circle').

20 English First, http://www.englishfirst.com/trt/tefl.html.

21 This is entitled 'Exploring English: Language and Culture'.

22 'English Skills a Key for Mobility and Employment In the Middle East and North Africa', *ICEF Monitor* (21 April 2015), http://monitor.icef.com/2015/04/english-skills-a-key-for-mobility-and-employment-in-the-middle-east-and-north-africa/.

23 English First. Teach English Abroad and Discover the World, http://www.englishfirst.com/trt/.

24 Travel. Taipei, http://www.travel.taipei/frontsite/en/cms/cmsAction.do?method=goCMSDetail&contentId=292&menuId=1030201.

25 See endnote 23 above. Further market information on developments in the language travel industry drawn on in this section is also available online at ICEF (28 April 2015), http://monitor.icef.com/2015/04/new-study-highlights-global-language-travel-trends-and-the-role-of-agents/.

26 European Study Tours website, http://www.euro-study-tours.co.uk/index.aspx?agid=325&gclid=CPX7nfmD_sgCFafnwgodwRoIvQ.

27 See Heller (2010).

28 This extract is taken from a posting by Gaider (14 January 2011) on the 'Official Fenris Discussion' thread on Dragon Age, http://forum.bioware.com/topic/155545-the-official-fenris-

discussion-thread/page-3?bioware=1&bwp=1, a role-playing phantasy video game series that was released in 2009, which has annually added new series packs.

29 Carpenter and Tolkien (1981), Letter 180.

30 The Klingon Language Institute is an organization that facilitates communication among Klingonists through publications, language proficiency certification and an annual conference, http://www.kli.org.

31 Liebl (2015), *Gamezone News* (26 March 2015), http://www.statisticbrain.com/call-of-duty-franchise-game-sales-statistics/. Call of Duty was first released in 2003.

32 Little Pim's language immersion method, https://www.littlepim.com/about/language-learning-kids-method/.

GLOSSARY

Bilingual (see also: multilingual)
- competence: an individual's ability to function in two languages, either from birth or with another language learnt subsequently. This can be equal (native-like) ability in both or native-like in one and functional or partial in the other.
- education: a type of education that involves two languages of instruction. Ideally, this should be additive (rather than subtractive), a process in which another language is gradually added to the mother tongue (or first language).

capital, human
knowledge and skills that enable individuals to perform labour so as to produce economic value. Here, language teaching and learning are seen as part of investment in human capital.

commodification
the process of turning something into an object for commercial use. Examples are when languages (and specific language skills) are used as a marketable product in translation services or in heritage tourism.

creole (see also: pidgin)
Creole languages are defined as expanded versions of pidgins. They are handed down through generations; in other words, they become mother tongues with native speakers. Creole languages are used widely, for example in the West Indies.

economics (of language)
study of the relationship between economic and linguistic variables, for example, the social rate of return for someone with bilingual skills. This approach can be used to identify, measure and evaluate benefits and drawbacks of specific language policy decisions.

language(s)

- additional/non-native: learning or knowing a language other than one's first (or native) language(s). These terms are used throughout this book instead of 'foreign' language, which can be ambiguous in multilingual societies such as Switzerland.
- constructed: languages that are created ones, either for mystical purposes (as by Hildegard von Bingen), transnational use (Esperanto) or fiction (Klingon in Star Trek or Na'vi in Avatar).
- first: normally acquired in early childhood (sometimes called mother tongue or native language). This may not be one's 'usual' language, which could in due course be a language that is acquired later in life (as a second or third language).
- minority/regional/national: different designations for languages that may be supported in a country in addition to an official language used for government.
- proficiency: one's level of skill in speaking, hearing, reading and writing a language.
- repertoire: a person's ability to interact, even imperfectly, in several languages in everyday settings. This may involve varying levels of proficiency in different languages and for different functions. Someone's repertoire can change over the course of a lifespan through acquisition of new languages.

lingua franca

a language that is used (often over an extensive area) by people who do not share a native language in order to communicate with one another. Originally, this term was used to designate a merged language that was employed in the Mediterranean by speakers of different and mutually unintelligible tongues, often for commercial purposes. This language (but not the term) has since disappeared. A more modern idea is Esperanto, but commonly nowadays, pre-existing languages (Arabic, English or Spanish) are used to bridge language differences.

literacy

someone's reading and writing skills in a language; multilingual literacy is an ability to move back and forth between several languages.

localization

here this is understood as the process of adapting the text relating to a product for a specific market. This is mainly done through translation and involves sensitivity to local cultures.

multilingual (used here synomymously with plurilingual)
- competence: an individual's ability to use several languages effectively, in writing and speaking (here used synonymously with plurilingual competence). See also under 'bilingual'.
- education: schooling that begins in one language (often the mother tongue) and then transitions to additional languages. Mother tongue–based multilingual education is promoted as a means of improving learning outcomes and expanding the reach of education while also promoting (often lesser-used) local languages.

multilingualism (used here synomymously with plurilingualism)
refers both to a situation in which several languages are spoken within a certain geographic area (for example, in Nigeria or in many cosmopolitan environments) and to the ability of a person to master multiple languages.

opportunity cost
the benefits an individual could have received by taking an alternative course of action, for example by learning Mandarin Chinese versus the programming 'language' Java.

pidgin (see also: creole)
a reduced language used to bridge a communication gap between speakers who have no other language in common. Typically developed by indigenous populations, these are based on the language of the former major colonial powers (e.g. Portuguese, French or Dutch) to facilitate communication for commercial exchanges. Some of these evolved into more complex creoles that have native speakers.

plurilingual (see multilingual)
plurilingualism (see multilingualism)
resources
a distinction is made here between hard resources (e.g. rare earths) and soft resources (e.g. someone able to speak more than one language).

return on investment (ROI)
this metric uses a cost–benefit analysis on investment, for example, in linking additional language skills with wage differentials.

supply and demand
this states the relationship between price and quantity of a commodity. For example, if there are few people skilled in a

particular language where there is a great need for that language, the income potential for someone able to offer the language will be pushed up.

value (economic and non-economic)

in economics, a distinction is made between the market (or direct) value and non-market (or indirect) value of a commodity or service. For example, the direct value of multilingualism is reflected in costs (e.g. of language services), wages (e.g. for someone with language skills) and prices (e.g. of producing product labelling in multiple languages); its indirect value can refer to such aspects as culture, identity or human rights.

utility

in economics, this is a measure of preferences over some set of goods and services. The concept presupposes that humans make rational choices in aiming for satisfaction from a product or service or a skill they acquire.

REFERENCES

Adams, J. N., Janse, M. and Swain, S., eds (2002), *Bilingualism in Ancient Society: Language Contact and the Written Text*, Oxford: Oxford University Press.

Amano, T., Sandel, B., Eager, H., Bulteau, E., Svenning, J.-C., Dalsgaard, B., Rahbek, C., Davies, R. G. and Sutherland, W. J. (2014), 'Global Distribution and Drivers of Language Extinction Risk', *Proc. R. Soc. B*, 273: 2127–33.

Anderson, B. (1991), *Imagined Communities: Reflections on the Origin and Spread of Nationalism*, rev. edn, London: Verso.

Angouri, J. and Strubell, M. (2013), 'Multilingualism in Companies', *Journal of Multilingual and Multicultural Development*. Special Issue, 34/6.

Baron, R. (2004), 'Barriers to Effective Communication – Indications From the Cockpit', Guest Editorial. *AirlineSafety.Com.*

Berthoud, A.-C., Grin, F. and Lüdi, G. (2013), *Exploring the Dynamics of Multilingualism: Multilingualism and Diversity Management*, Amsterdam/Philadelphia: John Benjamins.

Blackledge, A. and Creese, A. (2010), *Multilingualism: A Critical Perspective*, London/New York: Bloomsbury Publishing.

Bleakley, H. and Chin, A. (2004), 'Language Skills and Earnings: Evidence from Childhood Immigrants', *The Review of Economics and Statistics*, 86/2: 481–96.

Blommaert, J. (2010), *The Sociolinguistics of Globalisation*, Cambridge: Cambridge University Press.

Bostock, J. and Riley, H. T., eds (1855), *The Natural History: Pliny the Elder*, London: Taylor and Francis.

Bourhis, R. V., ed. (1984), *Conflict and Language Planning in Quebeq*, Clevedon: Multilingual Matters.

Bowden, H., ed. (1997), *The Histories: Herodotus* (Books I–IX), Rawlinson, G. (trans., 1858), London/Vermont: Everyman Library.

British Chambers of Commerce (2004), Impact of Foreign Languages on British Business.

Carpenter, H. and Tolkien, C., eds (1981), *The Letters of J. R. R. Tolkien*, London: George Allen & Unwin.

Chiswick, B. R. and Miller, P. W. (2007), *The Economics of Language: International Analyses*, London: Routledge.

Coulmas, F. (1992), *Language and Economy*, Oxford/Cambridge, USA: Blackwell.

Cummins, J. and Swain, M. (1986), *Bilingualism in Education: Aspects of Theory, Research and Practice*, London: Longman.

Curtin, P. D. (1984), *Cross-Cultural Trade in World History*, Cambridge/New York: Cambridge University Press.

Crystal, D. (2003), *English as a Global Language*, Cambridge: Cambridge University Press.

Deaux, G. (1969), *The Black Death 1347*, London: Hamish Hamilton.

DePalma, D. A., Hegde, V., Pielmeier, H. and Stewart, R. G. (2014), *Annual Review of the Translation, Localization, and Interpreting Services Industry: Common Sense Advisory*, Cambridge, MA: Lowell.

De Rachewiltz, I. (1972), *Papal Envoys to the Great Khans*, Stanford: Stanford University Press.

Edwards, J. (2012), *Multilingualism: Understanding Linguistic Diversity*, London: Continuum.

Erard, M. (2011), *Babel No more: The Search for the World's most Extraordinary Language Learners*, New York: Free Press.

European Union-DG VII (1999), *MARCOM Project: The Impact of Multicultural and Multilingual Crews on Maritime Communication* (Final Report Contract No. WA-96-AM-1181), Brussels, Belgium: A Transport RTD Program.

Extra, G. and Yağmur, K., eds (2012), *Language Rich Europe: Trends for Policies and Practices for Multilingualism in Europe*, Cambridge: Cambridge University Press.

Extramiana, C. and Van Avermaet, P. (2011), *Language Requirements for Adult Migrants in Council of Europe Member States: Report on a Survey*, Strasbourg: Council of Europe.

Frith, C. (2009), 'Role of Facial Expressions in Social Interactions', *Phil. Trans. R. Soc. B*, 364: 3453–8.

Gazzola, M. and Grin, F. (2013), 'Is ELF More Effective and Fair than Translation? An Evaluation of the EU's Multilingual

Regime', *International Journal of Applied Linguistics*, 23/1: 93–107.

Gladwell, M. (2009), *Outliers: The Story of Success*, London/ New York: Penguin.

Golden, P. B. (2011), *Central Asia in World History*, Oxford: Oxford University Press.

Grech, M., Horberry, T. and Koester, Th. (2008), *Human Factors in the Maritime Domain*, London: CRC Press, Taylor and Francis.

Grin, F. (2003), 'Language Planning and Economics', *Current Issues in Language Planning*, 4/1: 1–66.

Grin, F. and Vaillancourt, F. (1997), 'The Economics of Multilingualism: Overview and Analytical Framework', *Annual Review of Applied Linguistics*, 17: 43–65.

Grin, F., Sfreddo, C. and Vaillancourt, F. (2009), *Langues étrangères dans l'activité professionelle* (LEAP). Rapport final de recherché. Université de Genève.

Grin, F., Sfreddo, C. and Vaillancourt, F. (2010), *The Economics of the Multilingual Workplace*, New York/London: Routledge.

Heller, M. (2010), 'The Commodification of Language', *Annual Review of Anthropology*, 39: 101–14.

Hetherington, C., Flin, R. and Mearns, K. (2006), 'Safety in Shipping: The Human Element', *Journal of Safety Research*, 37: 401–11.

Hickey, S., 'Good Enough for Gates: Learn a Lingo by App', *The Guardian: Financial* (9 March 2015), p. 28.

Hogan-Brun, G., Mar-Molinero, C. and Stevenson, P., eds (2009), *Discourses on Language and Integration: Critical Perspectives on Language Testing Regimes in Europe*, Amsterdam: J. Benjamins.

Innis, J. (1950), *Empires and Communications*, Oxford: Clarendon Press.

Johnston, D. M. (2006), *The Historical Foundations of World Order: The Tower and the Arena*, Leiden: Martinus Njioff Publishers.

Kelly, N., DePalma, D. and Stewart, R. G. (2009), 'Language Services and the U.S. Federal Government. A detailed look at Uncle Sam's translation Spending Habits', *Common Sense Advisory*, Cambridge, MA: Lowell.

Keysar, B., Hayakawa, S. L. and An, S. G. (2012), 'The Foreign-Language Effect: Thinking in a Foreign Tongue Reduces Decision Biases', *Psychological Science*, 23/6: 661–8.

Latham, M. P., trans. (1958), *The Travels of Marco Polo*, Hammondsworth/Baltimore: Penguin.

Levitt, S. and List, J. A. (2008), 'Homo Economicus Evolves', *Science*, 319: 909–10.

Lewis, B. (2014), *Fluent in 3 Months*, New York: HarperCollins.

Lightfoot, L., 'MBAs Need to Teach Soft Skills', *The Guardian* (9 December 2014), p. 4.

Lindhout, P., Swuste, P., Teunissen, T. and Ale, B. (2012), 'Safety in Multilingual Work Settings: Reviewing a Neglected Subject in European Union Policymaking', *European Journal of Language Policy*, 4/2: 137–69.

Lo Bianco, J. (1987), *National Policy on Languages*, Canberra: Australian Government Publishing Service.

Lung, R. (2011), *Interpreters in Early Imperial China*, Amsterdam: John Benjamins Publishing.

Mahaffy, J. P. (2014), *The Empire of the Ptolemies*, Cambridge: Cambridge University Press.

Matras, Y. and Robertson, A. (2015), 'Multilingualism in a Post-Industrial City: Policy and Practice in Manchester', *Current Issues in Language Planning*, 16/3: 296–314.

May, S. (2001), *Language and Minority Rights: Ethnicity, Nationalism and the Politics of Language*, Harlow: Pearson Education.

McCants, A. E. C. (2007), 'Exotic Goods, Popular Consumption, and the Standard of Living: Thinking about Globalization in the Early Modern World', *Journal of World History*, 18/4: 433–62.

Page, T. E., Capps, E. and Rouse, W. H. D., eds (1928), *Procopius in Seven Volumes*, Books VII & VIII, London: William Heinemann.

Paul, J. (2013), 'Improving Communications with Foreign Speakers on the Shop Floor', *Safety Science*, 52: 65–72.

Pavlenko, A. (2006), *Emotions and Multilingualism*, Cambridge: Cambridge University Press.

Phillipson, R. (2009), *Linguistic Imperialism Continued*, London: Routledge.

Pinker, S. (1994), *The Language Instinct*, London/New York: Penguin.

Reisz, M., 'Language Degrees: When the Words are not Enough', *Times Higher Education* (11 December 2014), p. 12.

Ridler, N. B. and Pons-Ridler, S. (1986), 'An Economic Analysis of Canadian Language Policies: A Model and its Implications', *Language Problems and Language Planning*, 10: 42–58.

Saiz, A. and Zoido, E. (2005), 'Listening to What the World Says: Bilingualism and Earnings in the US', *The Review of Economics and Statistics*, 87/3: 523–38.

Siegel, J. (2008), *The Emergence of Pidgin and Creole*, Oxford: Oxford University Press.

Smith, D. E. and Karpinski, L. C. (1911), *The Hindu-Arabic Numerals*, Boston/London: Ginn and Company, Publishers.

Solomon, M. (2011), *Consumer Behavior: Buying, Having and Being*, London/New York: Pearson/Prentice Hall.

Tutt, D., Dainty, A., Gibb, A. and Pink, S. (2011), *Migrant Construction Workers and Health and Safety Communication*, Bircham Newton, King's Lynn: CITB-Construction Skills.

Uricuoli, B. and LaDousa, C. (2013), 'Language Management/ Labour', *Annual Review of Anthropology*, 42: 175–90.

Vaillancourt, F. (1996), 'Language and Socio-Economic Status in Quebec: Measurement, Findings, Determinants and Policy Costs', *International Journal of the Sociology of Language*, 121: 69–92.

Wheelis, M. (2002), 'Biological Warfare at the 1346 Siege of Caffa', *Emerging Infectious Diseases*, 8/9: 971–5.

INDEX